lions and tigers and nurses

A nursing novella about lateral violence

Also by Amy Glenn Vega

BROKEN HEART

amy glenn ega

lions and tigers and nurses

A nursing novella about lateral violence

Pritchett&Hull

Published by
Pritchett & Hull Associates, Inc.
3440 Oakcliff Road, NE, Suite 110
Atlanta, GA 30340

This novel is a work of fiction. Names, characters, places and incidents either are the product of the author's imagination or are used fictitiously. Any resemblance to actual persons, living or dead, events or locales is entirely coincidental.

ISBN 978-1-933638-43-0

Manufactured in the United States of America

For every nurse

ACKNOWLEDGMENTS

I have a great number of people to thank for making *Lions and Tigers and Nurses* a reality. First and foremost, there are several nurses that I must thank. They include the managers and peers who have nurtured and mentored me as a health care education professional over the years: Andrea Novak, Deborah Teasley, Barbara Allred and Suzanne Riley.

To Martha Griffin, I especially thank you for sharing the wisdom that you have gained through your impressive research and work in shielding new nurses from lateral violence. I appreciate how supportive and encouraging you have been of the idea for this story, and hope that Lions and Tigers and Nurses will meet and exceed your expectations.

Thank you to the real Laura Gallagher, nurse educator extraordinaire, who crafted many of the characters and situations featured in this story with me over lunch at a pier-top restaurant on a gorgeous, sunny day in South Carolina. The Laura Gallagher in this story has some of her same signature humor and enthusiasm, but in the end, simply doesn't do her real-life counterpart justice.

A very special thanks is due to Fran London, my colleague, friend, and writer-hero who took the time to read what I had written and said the magic words that started this journey: "This is worthy of publication. Go for it!"

Thank you also to Russet Hambrick, Cheri Smith, Lyn Keating and Karen Mantzouris at Southern Regional Area Health Education Center, as well as Mitzi and John Grey of Grey and Associates, Inc., and Kathleen Bartholomew, whose eyes were among the first to read this story and provide the feedback that helped make it better.

Thank you so much, Betty Westmoreland, for being the next person to believe in me and for being willing to take a gamble on a venture in publishing a completely new series of educational stories for nurses. Thank you to Ken Baumann, the most down-to-earth guru of the English language and brilliant editor in the world. And thank you, Cecily Shull, for your dedicated behind-the-scenes work, great eye for detail and fantastic taste in martinis. Words cannot express how appreciative I am of the hard work and support of everyone at Pritchett and Hull Associates, Inc.

Thank you to my wonderful family and friends, who have provided ideas, encouragement and promises that they will buy hundreds upon hundreds of copies of this book to share with everyone that they know. (I'm holding you all to it!)

To my mother and best friend, Karen Allen. She became my number one fan on the day that I was born, and still is to this day. I love you, Mom.

And last but certainly not least, I thank God, through whom all things are possible.

Dear nurse,

I'm not a nurse. Nor do I play one on TV.

But, I've had the privilege of working very closely with nurses for the past fifteen years. I have a very deep respect and admiration for the amazing things that nurses do every day to make our lives better.

There's a very unique culture among nurses. You have your own language, your own way of doing things, your own little quirks of the trade. There aren't many other professionals in the world who can so openly discuss tumors and ostomies while eating pizza for lunch. Or watch hospital dramas on TV while pointing out all of the inaccuracies in the show, and weeping over the storyline at the same time. You have guts of steel and hearts of gold.

Having worked closely with some of you in both clinical and academic settings, I've been in the position of an outsider looking in on this delightful world of yours. I've watched you struggle with an overwhelming workload that taxes not only your body and your mind, but your heart too. I've watched you perform miracles and save lives, and I've seen you humble yourself in prayer and embraces and tears when miracles are beyond your power. I've tried my hardest to figure out your inside jokes and I've marveled at your amazing sense of humor that can lighten even the darkest day. You are my heroes.

I am not a nurse, and doubt that I ever will be. I simply wasn't blessed with the special gifts and talents that it takes to be a caregiver, so I choose to stand back and leave that work to those who do it best - the folks like you. I am, however, an educator and a storyteller. My gift to you is that I can observe your laughter and your pain, as well as your daily struggles and victories, and assemble them into a story that can teach you something that will help you to become a more capable and knowledgeable nurse.

What follows on the rest of these pages is an educational story. I hope that it will not only train you, but entertain you; that it will not only teach you, but reach you. Self-study questions are provided at the end to help you assess your mastery of the information presented in the story, and group discussion questions are also provided to help you reflect on the story's lessons within a group of others who have read it.

I hope that this is a valuable and meaningful learning experience to you. Please share your thoughts with me at www.nursingnovellas.com. Thank you in advance for giving your time and attention to this story. It is the greatest compliment in the world to me.

Sincerely,

Amy Glenn Vega

"Any culture that has been oppressed will inevitably turn on itself."

Arlene Delaronde

EDUCATIONAL OBJECTIVES

Upon completion of this educational activity, the learner should be able to:

1) Define lateral violence
2) Discuss why lateral violence occurs among nurses
3) List the top ten behavioral manifestations of lateral violence in the workplace
4) Identify evidence-based verbal responses to laterally violent behaviors

Chapter 1
Miriam

Miriam Simpson was having the best dream.

It was her last day at work. After thirty-three years of devoted service to Dogwood Regional Medical Center, she was finally doing it. She was going to retire.

The elevator doors opened, and when Miriam stepped out onto the Medical-Surgical South nursing unit, the halls were lined with all of the nurses that she had ever worked with, all of the patients she had ever cared for and all of the family members that she had sat quietly in corners and laughed and cried and prayed with. All of them were there to congratulate her on thirty-three years of a job well done, and to wish her well in her retirement.

They applauded her as she walked down the hall toward the nurse's station. They threw confetti – which housekeeping would normally throw a fit over, but there were the housekeepers in the corner, smiling and waving at Miriam. Yes, confetti was okay, just for today. Just for Miriam.

Mel was there. Pretty, petite, with her perpetually youthful face and her long jet-black hair tied into a ponytail. She wrapped a red velvet cloak around Miriam's shoulders. It was so long that it dragged the floor as Miriam continued to walk.

And Brad was there too. Handsome young Brad, with his dirty blonde crew-cut hair and clean-shaven face, still looking like he belonged on active duty in the military. He bowed down to Miriam and handed her a golden scepter.

Behind the desk of the nurse's station sat Donna. Her hair pulled up into a matronly bun, her big brown eyes sparkling, and her smooth, cocoa-colored face beaming, as always. Such a kind face. Miriam was going to miss it. She was going to miss all of their faces.

Donna rose from her seat and lifted a fat, tasseled, very expensive-looking pillow toward Miriam. Upon it rested a glittering crown, made of solid gold, and crusted with precious jewels.

The applause grew louder. Miriam bowed down, and Mel stepped forward to lift the crown from the pillow to place it on her head.

"All hail Queen Miriam!" Someone shouted from behind her.

Turning to face her kingdom of admirers, she felt tears spring to her eyes. She waved her hands at all of them in a slow-motion beauty pageant style, as she boarded a chariot drawn by two white horses, waiting to escort her into retirement.

"All hail queen Miriam!" Shouted the crowd.

"Long live the queen!"

"God bless the queen!"

"All hail the queen!"

"Thit!"

Thit? Thought Miriam, as her eyes opened.

No longer in the kingdom of Med-Surg South, and no longer the crown queen of retirement from her nursing career, Miriam pushed up on her elbows and looked around the bedroom.

It was still dark, not quite time to get up just yet. Even without her glasses, she could see that the digital clock on her nightstand agreed. It was just a few minutes after four in the morning. And she was all alone in bed.

She sat up quickly.

"Where are you?" She cried out to her husband.

"Thit. Thit, thit, thit." Was the reply from somewhere on the floor on the other side of the bed.

She jumped out of bed to find her husband lying spread eagle on the floor.

"What do you think you're doing?" She cried out. "You know you can't get out of bed by yourself now. You have to wake me up. You have to let me help you!"

"Thit," he said again. It wasn't a real curse word, of course, just an attempt at one. But Miriam wasn't about to let him get away with it.

"Enough of that bad language. I won't have it in my house. I won't. Just because life has taken a hard turn for you doesn't give you cause to go around cussing up a storm like that, old man. Even if you can't say the word quite right."

She bent down and lifted him up, pulling him back into bed with her. "Are you hurt?" She asked, as she turned on the lamp on his nightstand and assessed him from head to toe.

He shook his head from side to side.

"Why were you getting up… did you need something?"

He shook his head again. "Ah juss foh-gah."

I just forgot, Miriam understood.

She guided him back down onto his back and positioned his head on the pillow. Then she shut off the light and returned to her side of the bed and snuggled up next to him, resting her head on his shoulder.

"Go back to sleep," she soothed him. "And don't forget anymore."

You can't do things the way you used to, Miriam almost said aloud, but stopped herself before she began the lecture once again that she had delivered so many times before. *No more getting out of bed for a glass of water while I'm asleep, no more going outside onto the deck at 4 a.m. to smoke your pipe, no more watching football and cussing at the TV in the middle of the night, no more getting out of bed for anything, at all, without waking me up.*

"Promise you won't forget. Do you hear me, old man?"

He sighed deeply. "Thit."

She kissed his forehead. "I know, honey," she said. "I know it's hard. But I love you, and I'm here for you. You've got to let me help you, dear. Now good night."

Miriam drifted back to sleep, but didn't return to the kingdom of Med-Surg South in her dreams. Instead, she found herself walking through the front door of her home, where she laid down her crown and her scepter, and threw her royal cloak across the sofa in the living room. Then she went to her husband, who was sitting alone in his wheelchair on the back porch. She wrapped her arms around his shoulders and hugged him tightly.

Chapter 2
Donna

Reeling with anticipation, Donna LeShay ripped open the envelope that she'd found on the kitchen table. It was addressed to her son, Sean, but she couldn't wait for him to open it himself.

She held the letter up above her head, admiring the watermark of the Old Tower on the University of North Carolina at Chapel Hill official letterhead. She took a deep breath before she read the body of the letter.

"Dear Sean," she read aloud, "Thank you for your interest in The University of North Carolina at Chapel Hill. We regret to inform you that your application for admission has not been accepted at this time." Donna's heart sank, but she continued.

"However, you remain a strong candidate for admission due to your record of academic success, your involvement in your community, and your demonstrated leadership capabilities. For these reasons, we have placed you on the wait list for admission." Donna sat down, gripping the letter tightly.

"In the event that a space becomes available for you, we will issue an official letter of acceptance and send an admissions packet to you in the mail. We anticipate finalizing our wait list admissions no later than August 12th of this year. Sincerely, Emmanuelle Grace, Director of Admissions."

Donna leaned onto the table, bracing herself on her elbows and clasped her hands together. "Oh dear Lord... please let Miss Emmanuelle Grace have grace on my boy Sean. Please Lord, please... let him get accepted. This has been his dream, Lord, all his life, to go to UNC, and to be a Tarheel. So please, righteous Lord, make a way for my baby. If it is in thy blessed will, dear Lord, please, let it be. In Jesus' name... Amen."

When she opened her eyes, she saw the other letter on the table, in the same size envelope that the one from UNC had arrived in. Only the return address on this one was a PO Box, and the sender was a long string of initials – NCCIM-R. Underneath the address, written in pencil: *Darius LeShay #087461.*

She knew the acronym NCCIM-R all too well. *North Carolina Correctional Institution for Men-Raleigh.*

Darius had only written her three times since he had gone back to prison eight months ago for possession with intent to sell – his second offense. Each time he had written, he asked for only one thing. Money. Not for a visit, not for a Bible, not for pictures of her, nor his brother Sean, nor his sister Jeanette, nor his late father, who had died of a heart attack at the age of 54. Darius had just turned fourteen.

She opened the letter, her nerves more on edge than they had been when she had opened the letter from UNC.

Dear Mama....

Donna felt a lump in her throat and felt the tears coming again.

I hope you and Sean and little Jeanie is doing ok. I'm fine. Look Mama I was wondering if you could do me a favor. I need some money right now. Real bad. I borrowed this guy's TV and I broke it so now I need some money to give him to get it fixed. So if you could send some please. I need like $200.

Love,

Darius

His handwriting was still so juvenile. Many of the letters were backward and upside down. His spelling and grammar were horrible. It was a letter only a mother could decipher.

She suddenly remembered sitting at that same table with him nearly twenty years ago in first grade, when his dyslexia first became apparent.

"Mama, what's wrong with me? All the kids in my class call me stupid. They say I can't read. Am I stupid, Mama?" Tears welled in his big, brown eyes.

"Don't you listen to those little troublemakers, Darius. There's nothing wrong with you. Your brain just works a little bit differently from everyone else's. But you are not stupid, baby, and don't ever listen to anyone who tells you that."

Donna's mind skipped forward to the day that Darius came home from his tenth grade English class, with a big red "F" marked at the top of the ten-page essay that he had spent his entire weekend writing. "Mrs. Kelly called me stupid, Mama. I got the lowest grade in the class. She held it up and showed everyone else before she gave me the paper, and she told me not to bother showing up for class anymore if I was going to insult her with work like this."

"Oh Darius, don't you listen to her, she doesn't know what she's talking about," Donna consoled him. "I'll be calling her for a parent-teacher conference first thing in the morning, and I'll let her know that nobody talks to my boy that way. Don't you listen to her, Darius."

Unfortunately, Darius was so traumatized by the experience that he took Mrs. Kelly's advice as an invitation to drop out of school and never went back. Donna argued with him daily to re-enroll and tough it out until he graduated, but he refused.

After a few weeks of daily shouting matches between the two of them, Darius packed a bag and left home. Where he went, Donna wasn't sure. It was nearly six months later when he came back home, flashing jewelry and designer clothes and high-dollar athletic shoes. Across the table, he slid a thick wad of cash to her and smiled with satisfaction.

"All those people who called me stupid should look at me now," he said, as his cell phone rang and a pager buzzed noisily in his pocket. "I'm finally a success. Did you ever think I'd be able to take care of *you*, Mama, and afford nice things for myself?"

Donna looked at him with fear and doubt in her eyes. "And where is all of the money coming from, Darius?"

He laughed softly. "You don't need to worry about that, Mama. Trust me. It's all good."

She took several deep breaths before she pushed the money

back to her son and asked him to leave. "Don't come back until you're an honest man, Darius."

It had only been about five years ago, yet it felt like a lifetime had passed since she'd last seen her son. She guessed that Darius hadn't meant for the letter in her hands to bring back so many painful memories, but nonetheless, her heart was breaking.

Donna cried as she ran her fingertips over the words that Darius had scrawled, knowing that writing this letter had probably taken hours worth of effort.

Jeanette, Donna's fourteen year old daughter, entered the room and immediately sensed that something was wrong. Hearing her mother's sniffles, she sat down across from Donna at the table. "Mom, what's wrong?"

Donna reached for a tissue and blotted her eyes. "It's Darius. He wrote us a letter."

"What did he say? Did something bad happen?"

"No, baby," Donna sniffled. "Nothing bad happened. I just miss him, that's all."

"I do too," Jeanette said softly. "What did he say in the letter?"

Donna quickly folded the paper and stuffed it back in the envelope. "Oh, he just said hello and that he's... okay," said Donna.

Jeanette forced a little grin. "That's good at least – that he's okay."

Nodding, Donna smiled back at her. "I suppose." She blotted her eyes again. "I just worry so much about Darius."

"You did the best you could, Mom. Darius is a grown up. He has to take care of himself now."

Donna nodded. "You're right. It doesn't stop me from being sad, though, and it sure doesn't stop me from worrying. A mama never stops loving her babies, even when they make mistakes. Even bad mistakes, like Darius made."

Jeanette stood and went to her mother's side and knelt down to hug her. "It'll be okay, Mom," she said. "Everything will be okay. Sean will get into college, and Darius, he'll be okay too. And me ..." Jeanette spun around and struck a pose, tossing her hair over her shoulder. "I'm going to be a star. I can sing, I can dance, and the camera loves me."

She framed her face with her hands and batted her eyelashes. "I'm going to be rich and famous and I'll buy us all a house in Beverly Hills. And you and me and Sean and Darius will live there and swim in our own in-ground pool every day, and throw parties every night."

Donna laughed. "You're my shining star already, baby girl. Always and forever. That'll never change. I don't need a fancy house and a swimming pool in Beverly Hills. I've got you, and that's enough."

"I love you, Mom."

"I love you too, Jeannie."

Thank God, Donna thought to herself. *Thank God that after twelve hours on my feet all day long, taking care of people who are sick and sore and sutured up, and supervising a unit full of nurses and dealing with all of their drama... thank God that I have someone to come home to that takes care of me.*

Chapter 3
Mel

Imelda Tagaro rested her head on the steering wheel of her aging Toyota Camry. At eleven years old, the body was more rust than vehicle, and the air conditioner only worked sporadically. Across the parking lot at McDonald's, she saw a shiny new Lincoln Continental – the one she used to drive - pull into a parking space.

Bruce had given it to her as a birthday gift two years ago, and he took it back exactly one year later when they divorced. She got the Camry, the two kids – Jenny and Michael – and her last name back.

And there he was behind the steering wheel of the Lincoln. The handsome young attorney she had met twenty years ago in a nightclub in the Philippines, where she was born and raised. She had just finished nursing school and had been planning to move to the United States anyway. She even had a ticket to come over on the boat with thirty other young Filipino nurses from her graduating class. The United States was a wide open adventure at that point, and she wasn't sure which state or which region, for that matter, she wanted to make her home.

Her whirlwind romance with Bruce made that decision very easy for her. He had just taken over the law practice of his recently retired father in Dogwood, North Carolina. Right in the middle of the state, it was three hours from the mountains, three hours from the coast. It was the perfect place to live, he had told her. With long, warm summers, mild winters and beautiful dogwood trees that bloomed in the spring.

There was a legend that the wood of the Dogwood tree had been used to make the cross on which Jesus was crucified. After his resurrection, the Dogwood tree's blossoms became the shape of a cross, and the centers of them tipped with nail prints – brown from rust, and red from blood. The center of the blossom was a crown of thorns. And it was because of this legend that she felt sure that meeting Bruce and following him to Dogwood, NC, was her destiny. Christ was calling her in that direction and she willingly followed.

The first few years after they married were bliss. Jenny was born thirteen months after their wedding, and Michael came along three years later. They were happy, for the longest time, and took lots of weekend and summer trips to the beach and to the mountains.

But on their tenth anniversary, Bruce didn't come home until 3 a.m. They'd had a knock-down drag-out fight that morning, when Mel had asked Bruce to take the day off, and he had replied a little too quickly that he couldn't waste a vacation day. He'd left the house in a huff, and Mel, feeling selfish and regretful, took it upon herself to make amends. She sent the kids to a babysitter, cooked Bruce's favorite dinner, lit candles and poured two glasses of wine. She poured them down the sink at 2 a.m. when Bruce called and said that he was still in the office and would be home late.

His long nights away from home became overnights away from home, and she saw less and less of him over the next two years. When he finally confessed the affair to her, she wasn't surprised. He swore that it was over, so after she cried, she forgave him, and they agreed to go to marriage counseling. They lasted another seven years together, and had some happy moments along the way, but things were never the same. It wasn't long after their nineteenth wedding anniversary, just before Mel's fortieth birthday, in fact, that Bruce sat her down and told her that he had fallen in love with another woman he had met over the Internet, and he wanted a divorce. Her name was Amanda, and ironically enough, she was a young nurse from the Philippines.

Mel had one question for Bruce. "Why?"

"Because I fell in love with her. Because she reminded me of you, the way you used to be when you were younger," was his reply. It was the closest that words had ever come to feeling like a slap in the face.

Mel went numb and didn't eat, speak or even sleep for a few

days. Then, she quietly and calmly regained her composure, went to the courthouse, filed for separation papers, and made a phone call to Bruce. "I want the kids. And my name back. You can have everything else."

She gave it all back, and he took it. The house, the summer condos at the beach and the mountains, the Lincoln, the country club membership, the boat, their wedding anniversary, her birthday and his name. She had no use for any of it anymore.

Still, there were things that she missed about Bruce. Mostly the way that he was with the kids – the way that he would smile at them and ruffle their hair when they were younger, the way that he would roughhouse with Michael as he got older and the way that he would tease Jenny about waiting on the front porch with a shotgun when the boys came over to ask her out on a date. In spite of his inability to be loyal to her, he had always been a good father.

"Hi Mom!" Michael bounded out of the Lincoln and raced to the Camry. He flung the passenger door open, crawled into the car and hugged her. He dragged into the car behind him a suitcase full of clothes from his weekend stay with Bruce. They had gone to see Jenny at Western Carolina University for Parent's weekend. Mel couldn't go because she was back to working weekends to make extra money now that Jenny was in college. So Bruce had offered to make the trip, and take Michael with him. He was more than happy, he told Mel, to journey out to the beautiful campus set in the mountains, for a long weekend that included a football game, a carnival on campus, dining out at great restaurants and probably a stay at a cozy hotel somewhere, with an indoor pool and Jacuzzi. Yes, Bruce was more than happy to go spend that time with Jenny, and of course bring along Michael. And Amanda.

There she was in the passenger's seat of the Lincoln. She waved to Mel with her left hand, flashing the big fat rock on her ring finger. She was as beautiful as the diamond on her hand; that was for sure. But Mel wondered how long Bruce would keep her around before he traded her in for a new model. Mel wanted to believe that she was over it all; that she had been strong enough to forgive and forget and move on with her life, but looking at Amanda sitting there next to Bruce stung her in a way that she never would have expected.

That's my car, she wanted to say to Amanda. *And that's my son that you just spent the weekend with, my wonderful boy. And that's my daughter, my smart, beautiful daughter that you sat next to and cheered with at the football game. And that's my once-husband sitting at your side. That's MY life that you stole.*

She wiped a tear from her eye as the Lincoln backed out of the parking lot and pulled away.

"Are you okay, Mom?" Michael asked.

"Yeah... I'm fine. You ready for school?"

Michael groaned. "I'm never ready for school," he replied. "Although it was kind of cool to spend Sunday night with Dad and Jenny and Amanda. Made the weekend seem longer. We had so much fun, Mom! I wish we could have stayed there forever."

Mel's heart ached. "I'm glad you had a good time," she said, as her cell phone began to ring. "You can tell me all about it after school today, okay?"

Reaching into her purse, she grabbed her phone. She recognized the number and answered it.

"Hey you... what's new?"

The voice on the other end of the line sounded groggy, almost sick. "Hi Mel," Brad replied. "Are you working today?"

"Yeah. I just picked up Michael and I've got to drop him off at school. I'll be in right after that. What about you?"

"Yeah. Let's get lunch together today. I need some advice right now."

Chapter 4
Brad

Brad Jackson awoke to unfamiliar surroundings.

Where am I? How did I get here? Am I safe?

His military training, piqued by his survival instincts, kicked in as his eyes darted around the room. He was alert and awake, but remained silent and still. Sudden movements could be deadly. Stealth was his friend.

His stomach growled loudly, and a wave of nausea overtook him. He wondered... had he been kidnapped? Drugged? Assaulted?

Brad focused his senses, struggling to make out his surroundings.

He was in a small, dark room, from what he could tell, lying on a carpeted floor. There was a foul, fishy smell on the floor. Somewhere outside, a dog barked.

Brad struggled to remember how he had ended up here.

His last memory was of his girlfriend of three years, Sue. They were having dinner at La Fiesta, his favorite Mexican restaurant. He was chewing on an enchilada when Sue brought up the dreaded subject again.

"Brad... are we ever going to get married?"

He felt his stomach flip flop, and he knew that it wasn't because of the guacamole he had eaten earlier.

"Sue… can we talk about this later?" He pleaded.

She pouted. "Look, Brad, all of my sisters are married. All of my friends are married. All except for Lucy, and she just got engaged. She just asked me to be her maid of honor at her wedding in eight months. I've been in twelve weddings since I met you, Brad. *Twelve.* And none of them have been mine." She dropped her face toward her lap and looked at her ringless left hand.

"This isn't a good time to talk about this, Sue."

As if on cue, the restaurant's three-man mariachi band entered the room and positioned themselves right next to Sue and Brad's table, immediately launching into a very loud rendition of "*La Cucaracha.*"

Thank God, thought Brad, drawing a ten dollar bill out of his wallet and placing it on the edge of the table to tip the musicians.

"It's never a good time, is it?" Sue cried out, over the loud music.

Brad smiled and shrugged. "What? Can't hear you!" he pointed to the mariachi band.

Sue reached into her purse and pulled out a twenty dollar bill, waving it in front of the musicians' faces. "*Ándale…* go away!" Sue shouted at them. The guitarist grabbed Sue's twenty and Brad's ten and scurried off in search of new victims to serenade.

Brad sighed. "Sue, come on. I love you. You know that. We just moved in together, didn't we? Both of our names are on the lease. Doesn't that prove I'm committed to you?"

Sue hesitated for a moment, and then shrugged. "I don't think so, Brad. All it proves is that you're responsible for half of the rent every month." Her tone was so chilly that Brad was sure that he saw frost forming at the edge of her mouth. "I keep asking you if you're ever going to be ready to commit to me. You keep dodging the subject. What am I supposed to do? Sit around and wait forever for you?"

Brad squirmed in his seat. "Sue… please. Do we really have to do this right now?"

"Apparently not," she said. "In fact, we don't have to do this *ever*, if that's what you want."

"Come on, Sue," Brad begged, as he waved his hand in the air, and the mariachi band came scrambling back to their table. "I just want to hear the band. Don't you?" Turning to the black-suited, sombrero-wearing musicians, he pleaded with his eyes for them to stay put. "Can you play *Piel Canela*, please?" He requested, digging in his pocket for more cash, and smiling in Sue's direction. "I'd like to dedicate this song to my girlfriend."

The guitarist in the middle began strumming as one of the other players grabbed for Brad's money. "Beautiful song for a beautiful lady," he said as he grinned broadly.

Sue's eyes grew wide and her nostrils flared. "Beautiful lady with a beautiful sofa for her boyfriend to sleep on," she growled.

Brad felt himself beginning to sweat. "Come on, honey," he shouted over the music as he reached for her hand. "Let's talk later, okay? Can't we just enjoy the music? And the food? Let's just enjoy the evening and talk later, okay?"

"*You* enjoy the music and the food," she hissed at Brad as she stood up from her seat. "I'm going home. It's obvious you don't want to hear anything that I have to say. You think our relationship is just a big joke!" Sue was yelling, and the mariachi band members looked at each other uncomfortably. They began to sing *Piel Canela* a little bit faster.

"Wait," Brad stood up with her. "You're not serious, are you? We've not even finished dinner yet. We've still got a whole pitcher of margaritas…"

Sue's eyes lit up. "Oh, you want margaritas? Great. Then have some margaritas!" She picked up the pitcher from the table and emptied it over Brad's head.

The mariachi band members revved up *Piel Canela* to double speed and began to inch away from Sue and Brad's table.

Gasping from the chill of margaritas sliding down his body, Brad stared at Sue in amazement. "Have you lost your mind?" He asked.

Sue suddenly looked sad. "I'm sorry, Brad, but I had to get your attention somehow. You can't keep ignoring me. I don't want to be just someone's girlfriend for the rest of my life. I want to get married, and I want to have a family. Not right this minute, but I at least need to know that you want the same things that I do. And if you don't, then you need to tell me now so I can move on."

The mariachi band didn't even bother to finish the song. The violin player said something in Spanish that probably would have translated into profanity in English, and the three of them bolted to another wing of the restaurant.

Brad took several deep breaths, but couldn't find the right words. He shook his head and shrugged.

"I guess that tells me everything I need to know," Sue said. She picked up her handbag and her keys, and headed for the door, leaving Brad marinating in salty green slush.

Sue stormed out of the restaurant with tears in her eyes, and Brad sank back down into his seat. Not knowing what else to do, he dipped a tortilla chip in hot salsa and crunched down on it, hoping that it would warm him up from the inside out. Then he reached for his cell phone.

He dialed his friend, Sam. Thankfully, he answered.

"Sammy... I need a favor."

"What's up?"

"Sue's throwing a temper tantrum again. She walked out of La Fiesta and left me here."

"Dude... I'm on the way." Sam hung up the phone.

Moments later, Sam showed up and joined Brad at his table.

They ordered a pitcher of beer and commiserated over the women in their lives.

"Women are nothing but trouble," Sam offered, as Brad patted himself dry with paper napkins.

"Sue wants to get married," he confided in Sam.

"I thought you just moved in with her."

"I did. We co-signed the lease for the new apartment."

"Marriage... lease... what's the difference?"
"Exactly."

"Want another beer?"

Later, they journeyed to Sam's house, where they shared several more beers and ordered a pizza that arrived forty minutes later than the promised arrival time, with anchovies instead of pepperoni. They played a basketball video game, drank more beer, and tried to get Sam's Rottweiler, Biff, to eat the pizza. He wouldn't touch it.

Then there was more beer. And more video games with more beer. And more beer. Then the room began to spin.

And that is where Brad's recollection of the prior night ended.

His eyes began to adjust to the darkness, just enough for him to make out his surroundings. His legs and feet were resting atop a beanbag chair, his head on a pizza box. A half-full beer can was wedged into his armpit.

A dog's bark broke the silence again.

"Shut up, Biff!" Sam yelled from the sofa across the room.

Brad's head felt as if it would explode. He sat up weakly, wondering if he should go vomit now or lay back down and wait a few minutes. Unfortunately, his days in the Navy were long past him. Throughout his military career, he'd benefited more than once from fluids administered intravenously by fellow corpsmen after episodes of heavy drinking. Without such an advantage in the civilian world, Brad began to believe that the horrible hangovers he now experienced were twice as bad to make up for all the ones he had missed out on. "I really gotta quit drinking," Brad groaned loudly.

"You and me both," Sam agreed, as he rose from the sofa and proceeded to kick beer cans aside to clear a path out of his living room. "Biff is barking to come in. I can't believe I drank so much that I left him outside last night. He hates sleeping in his doghouse."

"Well at least I'm not the only one in the doghouse," Brad mumbled. "If Biff needs a roommate, tell him to give me a call."

"Hey, mi casa es su casa," Sam offered. "Should you need a couch or a floor or whatever, Sammy's Ultimatum Inn is always open for homeless noncommittal men with angry girlfriends."

"Thanks," Brad said.

Taking a deep breath and fighting back the urge to vomit, Brad stepped outside to get some fresh air. He slunk down onto the top step of Sam's porch and rested his aching head in his hands.

He wondered if Sue was at home right now, packing his things, preparing to kick him out. Or maybe she was packing her own bags, planning to be the one to leave. Didn't she get it? He had just moved in with her. He loved her. Wasn't that enough of a commitment?

Then again, maybe she was right. They were different, he realized. Ever since he had grown up and left home as a young adult, he had lived his life on the edge. Four years traveling the world as a medical corpsman in the Navy, and another five years working as a paramedic first, then as a nurse, had taught him that life was short, and nothing ever stayed the same. Live hard, die hard, that was his motto. So he worked hard, and he partied even harder.

Sue, on the other hand, saw the world through rose colored glasses. She worked at Hallmark, selling greeting cards, scented candles, Harry Connick, Jr. CD's and figurines of cutesy kittens. The eternal optimist and beauty queen, all she ever asked anyone for was world peace, and she meant it.

Brad did adore her. She was good for him in a lot of ways. She gave him a sense of balance and stability in his life, and he had seen more than once the value of being in a relationship with someone different from himself. But the thought of settling down and marrying someone who was his polar opposite scared the living daylights out of him.

He recalled a prior argument they'd had not too long ago. Sue had accused him of being immature. Partying too much. Not acting like a responsible adult. Not wanting to grow up, settle down and commit to anything.

What does she know? He thought to himself, as he involuntarily leaned forward and vomited.

Okay… so maybe she was right on the money with her accusation about too much partying. But as far as her questioning his commitments, she was way off target, and he resented it.

If only she could spend a day at work with him and see how committed he was to his patients and what a good nurse he was, she'd surely cut him some slack. He loved taking care of people, and knowing that he was able to bring comfort and healing to a person in need was the most rewarding feeling he'd ever known. It meant the world to him, and he knew that he was good at it. *Great* at it. He willingly worked holidays, nights and weekends, fought for extra shifts, and stayed on the unit long after he clocked out. He just loved being a nurse.

"So why not just go to medical school and become a doctor?" People would ask him all the time.

"Because I'm a nurse," he'd reply. He felt that no other explanation was required, and so he never offered one.

And then he wondered, for a moment, if maybe that's why he didn't want to marry Sue. He'd already met the love of his life, and it was his job. Whether she understood that or not, he knew that she would never be content to play second fiddle in his life.

Brad finished throwing up, took several deep breaths, and resisted the urge to cry out.

"Mommy," he still whimpered, but only loud enough that he could hear it.

When he felt somewhat recovered, he reached into his pocket for his cell phone. He pressed number 3 on his speed dial.

"Hi Mel," he said. "Are you working today?"

Chapter 5
Haylie

Haylie Evans shifted from one foot to the other.

"Stay still," her mother scolded, "or we'll never get the alternations just right."

Haylie's sister, Isabel, was getting married in less than three weeks. Isabel had always been a wonderful big sister – sweet, supportive, and every bit as much of a friend as a sibling. However, since she had gotten engaged last year, she had become a complete bridezilla. Moody, demanding and indecisive were the new words that Haylie used to describe her sister.

Late last night, after a fit of crying and browsing through bridal magazines, Isabel decided on a whim that she didn't like her bridesmaid dresses anymore, and that she had to change them. She called all of her bridesmaids in the middle of the night and demanded that they bring their dresses back to the bridal shop first thing in the morning to be altered.

Haylie, being the maid-of-honor, was informed sometime after one o'clock in the morning, after all of the other bridesmaids had been called. Isabel burst into her bedroom, woke her up in the middle of a peaceful sleep, and told her to set her alarm for six o'clock in the morning.

Now, while she stood as still as she could in her three-inch high heels, the hem of her maid-of-honor dress was being taken up by twelve inches. Isabel had decided that floor-length gowns were just too formal for a four o'clock wedding.

Haylie yawned and resisted the temptation to shift her weight again from one foot to another. "This is nuts, Mom. I have tons of other things I need to be doing today. Isabel's being very inconsiderate."

"I know," her mother agreed from the corner of the room, " but Isabel's big day is coming up soon. Let's just grin and bear it, and it will all be over shortly."

"I sure hope so." Haylie looked at her watch impatiently. "You know, I'm supposed to be at the hospital in a little less than an hour."

"Can't you call them and tell them you're going to be late?"

"No Mom, I can't. This is my first real job, and I'm not going to make a bad impression by showing up late on the first day. They've got a ton of stuff for me to do, you know. I'm supposed to go in to Human Resources today and get my picture taken for my name badge, fill out the benefits forms, take a drug test, get signed up for orientation classes, all that stuff… "

"Well, do what you must, but you know what I've always said. Family should come first."

Haylie moaned. "Family DOES come first for me, Mom, and it always will. If Isabel was laying in the hospital on her deathbed and needed a kidney to survive, I'd drop everything that I was doing and give her one of mine. But this isn't about a kidney; it's about taking a few inches off the hem of a perfectly good dress. A dress that Isabel decided long ago would be just fine for me to wear in her wedding. It's not my fault that she changed her mind last night, and I'm certainly not going to risk making a bad impression at my new job just to appease her. I won't be late, Mom. Sorry."

Her mother pouted. "Still, your sister's happiness should be important to you. Every girl's wedding day should be the most perfect day of her life. After all, you only get married once, and it's forever."

"Yes, I remember. You've told me as much before. Like four years ago at Isabel's first wedding."

"Don't bring that up, Haylie. This is Isabel's fresh start. Lots of people get divorced. She was just too young and married the wrong person. But this time, it's going to be forever. I can just feel it in my bones."

Resisting the urge to say something mean, Haylie kept quiet.

"I hope to see you walking down the aisle yourself, before too much more time passes, Haylie…"

"Mom… don't start, not now."

"What? I want grandchildren. And lots of them. Isabel's thirty-three years old already, and you're twenty-two. If you two don't get started soon…"

"Mom! Enough already!" She looked at her watch again. "I need to get going anyway." She wiggled out of her dress, letting it fall to the floor.

The seamstress struggled to collect the garment, handling it with the greatest of care, as not to rearrange the pins she had used to mark the hemline. "Sorry about the alterations. Just make your best guess, and I'll be okay with it. I have to go to work now." Haylie apologized, as she pulled on a brand new set of scrubs.

"And what is it that you do?" The seamstress asked.

Haylie smiled. "I'm a nurse," she said. "Or I'm going to be in about an hour, anyway. I just graduated from nursing school a few months ago, passed my boards last week, and got hired by the hospital on Friday. I start work today."

"Oh, that's fantastic," said the seamstress. "I keep hearing that there's a huge shortage of nurses here in North Carolina."

"Oh, there's a shortage all over America," Haylie responded.

The seamstress carefully hung Haylie's gown back on its hanger. "In that case, don't worry about the bridesmaid gown. I think I can do just fine with the alterations. I've got to have surgery in a few weeks, so you go tell all of those nurses to take good care of me."

Haylie nodded. "You bet I will! And if you end up on Med-Surg South, then I just may get to be your nurse."

"Well good luck," the seamstress said with a smile. "Go do a great job. Make your mom proud!" She winked at Haylie's mother, who was hovering in front of Isabel's bridal gown hanging on a rack in the corner of the room.

"I'd be proud to see *both* of my daughters settling down and getting to work on making some grandchildren for me." Haylie's mother sighed. She turned to her daughter with worry etched into her face. "Do you even have a date to the wedding?"

"I'm in the wedding – maid of honor – remember? I didn't think I had to have a date if I was in the wedding party."

"You'll need someone to dance with at the reception."

"I'll dance with the best man and the groomsmen."

"They're all married, and they'll all be dancing with their wives."

"So I'll dance by myself."

"Please find a date. You don't have to marry him and have children with him, but at least show up with someone to dance with you at the reception."

"Fine," Haylie said. "I'll get right on it, I promise. But for now, Haylie Evans, RN, is reporting for work."

Chapter 6
Dogwood Regional Hospital
Med-Surg South
Monday

The day started like any other on the Medical-Surgical South Unit of Dogwood Regional Hospital in Dogwood, North Carolina.

It was a Monday morning, but the day of the week meant very little to most of the RN's who worked here. Unlike folks who worked the 9 to 5 in an office or a cubicle, with evenings, weekends and holidays off, Monday mornings for nurses were no different than Wednesday evenings or Saturday nights. There were patients in beds around the clock, all days of the week.

Only this Monday morning was a little bit different, as a new nurse was starting work here today.

Donna had printed out a banner and posted it on the break room wall.

WELCOME HAYLIE!

"Haylie?" Miriam frowned. "Are you sure that's how you spell it?" She asked Donna.

"Yes, that's how it's spelled."

Mel looked at the banner. "She must be really young... a new grad, I bet. I kind of like that spelling. It's unusual. Pretty."

"Oh nothing unusual about it," said Miriam. "Aren't they all named Haylie these days? Or some variation of it?"

"Well, we do get an occasional Taylor," said Brad, as he entered the break room.

Miriam sighed. "When I was twenty-something, I had never heard of a Haylie or a Taylor. What happened to Lindas and Sharons and Barbaras and Miriams?"

"Different generation, different names that are popular," offered Donna.

"So what's the new Haylie like?" Mel asked.

Donna smiled. "Well, you guessed right, she's a new grad," said Donna. "Very blonde, very pretty. Seems sweet-natured. I met her on Friday. HR brought her up to the unit to take a look around."

"What did she think?" Miriam asked.

Donna took a deep breath. "Well, the expression 'deer caught in the headlights' comes to mind…"

"Hmmmf," Miriam grunted. "Just what we need up here. More green nurses to teach and train. I wonder why they even bother making them go through nursing school anymore. They may as well just pull people off the street and send them up here in scrubs. It would take no less time and effort to train a complete layperson than it would to train a new grad."

Donna shook her head. "That's enough Miriam. Don't unload all that negativity onto my new nurse when she gets here."

"Oh, I won't. Trust me, I'll be staying as far away from her as I can get."

"I don't think so," Donna said. "I'm assigning you to precept her."

It was almost possible, in that moment, to hear a pin drop.

Brad and Mel shot each other a glance and quickly backed out of the room.

"I don't think so," Miriam began. "Not me. Anyone but me."

"Miriam, please. Mel is working extra shifts and has a lot on her plate right now. And Brad isn't quite ready to precept – I want him to get some more experience under his belt. You've been here for thirty-three years and you know this job and this unit like the back of your hand. I need you to help out with this new nurse and get her up and running. You're the absolute best person for the job, Miriam, and I'm counting on you."

Miriam looked away and sighed.

"Please?" Donna begged.

"As if I had a choice," Miriam relented. "Fine."

"Please… do keep a positive attitude," Donna encouraged her.

"I'll try. You know how frustrated I get with new grads, though. I don't know why you never let me precept the traveling nurses or the temp nurses or the refresher nurses…. you always give me the brand new ones."

"Because they're the ones that need you the most."

"Hmmf," Miriam grunted. "You know, Donna, there was a day when I was the nurse manager on this unit, long before your time. And I stepped back. I went back to being a floor nurse because I'm trying to wind down and get ready for retiring sometime in the next few years. But it kind of defeats the purpose when I'm having to precept these brand-new nurses. It's a lot of time and effort."

"I know that," she agreed. "But honestly, you'd be doing it whether you had the official title of preceptor or not. All nurses are teachers, Miriam. All nurses are mentors. And I specifically want you to work with Haylie because I know that you'll be leaving us someday soon. We need for all of your skills and experience and wisdom to stick around here after you're gone, and this is how you leave your legacy – you pass all of that on to the new nurse coming in."

"Which I guess would be me," spoke a youthful, high-pitched voice from the doorway of the break room. Donna and Miriam turned in that direction and focused their attention on the young woman standing in the doorway. "Hi… I'm Haylie," she said, addressing Miriam, as she had already met Donna the Friday before.

Miriam arched her eyebrows and nodded in her direction. "I'm Miriam," she said coolly. "I guess I'm going to be your preceptor. And your first lesson of the day – don't invite yourself into other people's conversations. It's rude."

Haylie's face fell into an expression of confusion.

Donna swatted at Miriam's arm. "Oh, she's just kidding, Haylie. Welcome. We're glad you're here."

Miriam pretended to smile in order to satisfy Donna, but narrowed her eyes to make her true feelings clear to Haylie. "Yes, welcome."

"Come with me, Haylie. I want to introduce you to the other nurses working first shift." Donna led Haylie to the nurse's station, where Mel was typing on the computer and Brad was talking on the phone.

"This is Haylie," Donna said to both of them.

Mel looked up and smiled, extending her hand to Haylie for a handshake. "I'm Imelda," she told her. "But everyone calls me Mel. You do the same."

Brad smiled and dropped the handset of the phone onto his shoulder for a brief moment. "I'm Brad. Great to meet you."

"Nice to meet all of you as well," Haylie replied. "I'm really excited to be here!"

"Super!" Donna exclaimed. "Let's go ahead and get you started. Your first patient is in bed 4-B. I'd like for you to go and meet her."

***

"Hi... Mrs. Reynolds?   My name is Haylie and I'm your nurse today."

Doris Reynolds, an eighty-eight year old woman with bleach-blonde, hot rollered hair, penciled eyebrows, and gaudy green clip-on earrings sat up in her bed, eyeing Haylie up and down.

"You're too skinny," she said to Haylie. "Are you one of them anorexics? Don't eat no food, starving yourself to look like a movie star? Or are you bulimic? I used to work with young girls your age. I know all about anorexics. And bulimics. I'm a retired schoolteacher."

She had a southern accent, reminiscent of Scarlett O'Hara, the kind that made the word "schoolteacher" sound like "schoolteach-a."

"No ma'am. I'm not anorexic or bulimic. I'm just very thin. I actually eat a lot. I just don't gain weight."

Mrs. Reynolds arched one artificial eyebrow and shook her head. "You never know," she said. "You young girls these days... you do all kinds of horrible things to your bodies."

"Well..." Haylie said, trying very hard to remain polite and professional, "how about we talk about you right now? I see in your chart that you got bitten by ants on your left foot and it turned into cellulitis.

Can I take a look at that foot and see if you're doing better?"

Mrs. Reynolds peeled back her sheet. Haylie somehow wasn't surprised to see bright red toenail polish on both of her feet. The left foot was quite swollen and red, and a bit warm to touch, but didn't look threatening.

"Your foot looks good, Mrs. Reynolds. I think the antibiotics that you're getting are working well. I'll be checking on you throughout the day. I think we'll see some of the swelling go down as the day goes on."

The patient looked at Haylie suspiciously. "Did you read the rest of my chart?"

"Well, I read most of it. The important stuff, anyway."

"Oh," Mrs. Reynolds said. "I just was wondering, because you didn't check the bottom of my feet like the other nurses always do. And you haven't asked me anything about my sugar."

"Sugar? You have diabetes?"

The arched eyebrow went down, and the other one went up. "It's in the chart. You should have read it. That's why my doctor put me in the hospital. He's worried about my feet. Because of my sugar."

Doct-a. Sug-a. The retired schoolteach-a's accent was grating on Haylie's nerves.

"Well, thank you for pointing that out to me, Mrs. Reynolds. That certainly makes sense that your doctor would want to hospitalize you and keep a close watch on your foot for a little while. So why don't you let me take another look at your feet?"

With a loud sigh, Mrs. Reynolds made her disapproval of Haylie's nursing skills very clear. "Thought you'd never ask."

Oooh. So sarcastic for a little old lady, thought Haylie. In nursing school, all of the little old ladies that they had talked about in their case studies were either sweet and kind, or else demented. Haylie hadn't been prepared for a cynical, judgmental diva.

"How long have you been a nurse, anyway?" Mrs. Reynolds asked.

About five minutes, actually, Haylie avoided saying aloud.

"Well... let's just say I'm very new."

Mrs. Reynolds grunted. "Just a child," she said. "Just a child. I come in to the hospital on my deathbed after a bunch of fire ants almost killed me, and they give me a child to watch over me."

I'm just a child, and you're just a drama queen, thought Haylie.

She leaned over to look at Mrs. Reynold's feet. They looked fine from the top. Leaning over a little farther, she peered at them from the bottom.

"Oh my Lord!" Mrs. Reynolds shrieked.

Haylie jumped back, startled by her patient's cry. "What's wrong?"

Mrs. Reynold's mouth gaped open. Her eyes were wide with shock. "You're tattooed."

Haylie's face turned beet red. "You saw that?"

"When you bent over my bed, your shirt raised up a bit, and I saw it. I saw that hideous tattoo on your bottom."

Hideous? It's a butterfly! What's hideous about a butterfly? Haylie wondered.

"It's not on my bottom, Mrs. Reynolds. It's on my lower back. And I'm sorry if it offends you."

"What wrong with you? Respectable young ladies don't mark up their bodies like that! I can't even believe that Dogwood Regional hired you. They must be truly desperate for nurses these days! Now you get out of my room before I call the hospital administrator and have you fired."

"Mrs. Reynolds, I'm really sorry –"

"Young lady," she said, her voice suddenly dropping in pitch, "Please… go get me a proper nurse. I don't need a schoolgirl taking care of me."

Feeling as if she had been slapped in the face, Haylie spun around to leave…

And came face to face with Miriam. There she stood in the doorway, frowning and shaking her head. "Go to the nurse's station," she said in a low voice, while rolling her eyes and shaking her head from side to side.

Haylie fled the room, knowing that if she had a tail it would surely be tucked between her legs.

What in the world did I do wrong? It's just a tattoo! Everyone's got them nowadays! Don't they?

At no point during the hiring process had Dogwood Regional ever told Haylie that tattooed nurses were not allowed to work at their hospital. As far as she knew, she wasn't breaking any rules or doing anything horrible, so just because Mrs. Reynolds flipped out over it wasn't any cause for Miriam to act that way.

Why didn't Miriam stick up for me? Wondered Haylie. *What's the point of having a mentor if she's just going to undermine me and chase me away every time I need help? She should have helped me!*

But no, she had sent her out of the room. And rolled her eyes and shook her head.

Off to a great start already, way to go... Haylie thought to herself.

***

In the break room, Donna sat between Haylie and Miriam.

"What's the problem, ladies?"

Miriam sighed. Her face was crimson red. She looked every bit as angry as her deep voice sounded when she finally spoke. "Haylie just had a confrontation with a patient."

Haylie was taken aback. "I wouldn't call it a confrontation," she defended herself. "I was leaning over to look at Mrs. Reynold's feet, and my shirt slipped forward a little bit, I guess. Anyway, she saw the tattoo that I have on my lower back and she flipped out. She started yelling at me, saying she was going to get me fired... just for having a tattoo! I didn't do anything wrong."

Miriam sneered. "That's not what I heard. When I talked to Mrs. Reynolds, she told me that the real reason that she was upset was because you didn't check her feet correctly. She's a diabetic. You ALWAYS check the bottom of their feet. That should have been one of the first things that you learned in nursing school."

"I did learn that. I just didn't realize that she was diabetic at first."

"You should have read her chart."

"Well, I did…"

"Well you missed the most important part."

Donna held her hand up, waving it as if it were a referee flag. "Okay," Donna intervened. "There are a couple of different problems here."

"Just a couple?" Miriam said under her breath.

Donna shot Miriam a dirty look, and then turned her attention to Haylie. "It is very important for you to read your patient's chart. And talk to the other nurses, too. The nurses who have been caring for Mrs. Reynolds before you can tell you what you need to know about her." Then she turned to Miriam. "And that would be you, in this case. Did you mention to Haylie that Mrs. Reynolds is diabetic?"

Miriam shook her head from side to side. "No," she said. "I shouldn't have to. It's in the chart."

Donna's voice was firm. "You should have shared that information with Haylie."

Miriam crossed her arms and leaned back in her seat, looking very self-righteous. "Look… she needs to learn to either sink or swim, just like I had to when I was a brand new nurse. Just like we *all* had to. We've all been there, Donna. I'm just trying to mentor Haylie, not spoon-feed her. I'm trusting that she has a basic level of knowledge and skills and instead of me hovering over her shoulder every single minute and telling her what to do, I'm just trying to give her guidance."

"Well I want you to 'hover' a little bit more, Miriam. I want you to share important information with Haylie about patients." Then she turned to Haylie. "And as far as the tattoo issue, the fact that you have a tattoo on your lower back is fine, but I do expect you to keep it covered."

"But I do. My scrubs cover it. It's just that I leaned forward and my shirt slipped up a little bit…" Haylie felt as if she were under attack.

"I know," Donna said, "But you're going to be doing *a lot* of moving around Haylie. You'll be bending over, lifting patients, reaching for equipment… this is a very physical job. I'm going to suggest that you go up a size in your scrubs. A longer hem will help to cover your tattoo."

Haylie looked down at her uniform. "But this is the right size for me. If I go up a size in scrubs, they'll be baggy and loose."

"Well you're not here for a fashion show. That's how they're supposed to fit," Miriam said. Haylie resisted the urge to say how snug Miriam's scrubs looked on her rather large rear end. Haylie guessed that Miriam's scrub size was at least a 3X, and even then, she was practically busting the seams of both her shirt and her pants.

Donna looked at Miriam with scolding eyes. "That's enough, Miriam," she said. "There's no need for sarcasm. We need to finish up this discussion and end on a positive note."

"What about Mrs. Reynolds?" Haylie asked. "She pretty much hates me, so I don't think I should go back in there."

"You can trade a patient with Miriam," Donna said.

Miriam grinned. "You can take Mr. Crowell," she said.

"That's fine," Donna agreed. "Please give Haylie a report on Mr. Crowell. Tell her everything – and I do mean *everything* – that she needs to know in order to take care of him. And Haylie, read Mr. Crowell's chart. I want you to really take the time to look it over. Not just the narrative sheet. Check out his labs too. Look at everything."

***

At lunch in the hospital cafeteria, Brad stared down his plate of Buffalo wings.

"What's the matter?" Mel asked. "You haven't touched your food. I know you love wings, so I'm worried."

"I guess I'm just not hungry," Brad replied. "All of this drama with Sue is wearing me out."

Mel finished the last bite of her salad and leaned back in her seat. "Jeez, I'm sorry, Brad. I wish I knew what to tell you. What do you think you should do?"

He shrugged. "Honestly, I don't know. I don't want to break up with Sue, but I'm not ready to get married yet, either."

"It sounds like she's ready, whether you are or not."

"Yeah. And I don't know what to do about it. The problem is, I don't know if I'll ever be ready."

Mel sighed. "I don't know what to say, Brad. Have you considered… maybe Sue's not the one for you?"

He nodded. "Maybe so. Or maybe she is, and I just don't want to be the kind of guy who settles down and gets married and has a family. Maybe I just want to have a steady girlfriend for the rest of my life."

"Well, that's convenient for you, but unless you find a woman who is willing to accept being just a girlfriend for the rest of her life, you may be out of luck. And I just don't think that Sue is willing to compromise what she wants just to stay with you."

"So what do I do, Mel?"

She reached across the table and squeezed his hand. "I don't know. I realize I promised you some good advice, but I honestly don't think that there's much that you can do. I think that Sue is making the decision for you. She's made it clear that she's ready to move on, and although you're upset with the thought of losing her, it's not upsetting enough for you to make a commitment to her."

He nodded again. "I guess it's just not meant to be."

"It could be worse," Mel offered. "Better that you find out now, than nearly twenty years into a marriage, after your partner has cheated on you, broken your heart, burned up all of your trust, and finally, leaves you for someone they met over the Internet…"

Brad squeezed her hand back. "Sorry, Mel. I wish you'd never had to go through all of that."

"You know why I left my home and came here, Brad? I came because I thought that God had given me a sign, that this is where I was supposed to make my home and live my life. All because of the legend of the Dogwood. I thought that this is where I was called to be."

"Well, maybe it was. Maybe you are meant to be here. Maybe it just took Bruce to get you here."

"I doubt it. I left behind all of my family and my friends and now here I am, alone."

"You're not alone. You've got Jenny and Michael and me." Brad smiled at her. "Life stinks sometimes, but overall, it's not so bad having friends like you. You're like the big sister I never had and I don't know what I'd do without you."

She smiled back. "I hear you, little brother."

***

Haylie carried her tray into the dining hall, relieved to be away from Miriam for a short while. Her first day had gotten off to a rough start, and it was only halfway over.

Glancing around the dining hall, she spotted two familiar faces – Mel and Brad. She moved in their direction, hoping to join them, but noticed that they were smiling and holding each other's hands across the table.

Looks like there's no need for a third wheel, thought Haylie, and found a small table for herself.

So far, Miriam hated her. Brad and Mel appeared to be a cozy couple, and Donna seemed sweet most of the time, but was clearly the boss and reminded Haylie a lot of her own mother. She had hoped that she would be able to make some new friends at work, but it wasn't looking likely.

Biting into her cheeseburger, she wondered if she'd have to eat lunch alone every day at work.

That would really stink, she decided.

***

On her way home from her first day at work, Haylie stopped by the uniform supply store and picked up a new pair of scrubs. A size larger than her true size.

It had been a hard first day.

Miriam, it seemed, was out to get her.

Her first and only patient had screamed at her and had threatened to have her fired.

None of the other nurses had gone out of their way to be friendly to her.

And she'd already gotten into trouble with her boss for wearing scrubs that were her correct size, which was apparently a size too small in the world of nursing.

Still, she was determined to keep a positive attitude.

Everyone hates Mondays, don't they? Haylie thought, as she forced herself to smile.

Tomorrow would be a better day. Whether the patients and the other nurses on Med-Surg South wanted it to be a better day or not, Haylie was going to make it a better day.

Chapter 7
Tuesday

That morning, Haylie stopped by the bakery and bought a dozen donuts, which she proudly placed on the break room table when she arrived at work that morning.

A peace offering.

Hopefully Miriam liked donuts. Judging by the size of her rear end, Haylie assumed that it was a safe bet.

Maybe Donna liked donuts too. And hopefully she'd notice that Haylie was wearing bigger, baggier scrubs that day, and maybe, just maybe, she'd lighten up on her today.

And hopefully Brad and Mel liked donuts too. Maybe they'd see that Haylie was just trying to fit in and make a few friends, and maybe they would invite her to lunch with them today.

Haylie got a little nervous when she realized that her good day was dependent on a dozen donuts and lots of maybes.

But still, she was determined to make Tuesday better than Monday had been.

At the nurse's station, she found Miriam studying a patient's chart.

"Good morning, Miriam," Haylie said cheerfully.

"You're late," Miriam said, not looking up from the chart.

Haylie looked at her watch. Indeed, she was late. By three

minutes. *Lighten up, Miriam!* She thought to herself.

"Oh… sorry. It's just that I stopped by the bakery and picked up some donuts for everyone on the way to work. So if you'd like to have one, feel free."

Miriam kept her nose in the chart. "Mr. Crowell just pressed his call bell. You need to go see what he wants."

So much for that plan, thought Haylie. *Just stay positive, stay positive…*

She entered Mr. Crowell's room.

"Good morning," she said. "My name is Haylie. I'm going to be your nurse today. Is there something I can do for you?"

Mr. Crowell looked away from the television and faced Haylie. His thick gray hair was sticking straight up on his head, as if he had literally been yanking and pulling on it, and he had tears in his eyes. "I'm in terrible pain," he said. "I need something. Quick."

Haylie stepped closer to his bed and checked the bag of fluid connected to his IV line. "You've got a PCA pump, Mr. Crowell. See that little wand in your hand. Just press the button whenever you feel like you need pain medication."

"What's PCA?"

"Patient Controlled Analgesia. It means you can give yourself medication as you need it."

"Oh, this," he said, looking down at the device in his hand. "I've been pressing this button until my thumb is sore. I should have overdosed myself on medicine by now, but it's just not enough."

"It will only give you a certain amount over a period of time. It won't let you overdose. But if you need something stronger, I can call the doctor."

Quickly growing agitated, Mr. Crowell grabbed the IV and pulled it out of his hand. Blood splashed onto his sheet and his gown. "There's nothing in there – you aren't giving me anything for pain! I'd be able to feel it if you were!" He struggled to get out of bed. "Pills," he cried out. "I want pills! There's nothing in that bag of fluid… nothing but salt water! Where's the pain pills? I'll get them myself if I have to!"

Startled, Haylie pressed the call button.

Miriam rushed into the room. "Mr. Crowell, what's the problem?"

"I need pain pills! Please!"

Miriam saw that he had pulled the IV out of his hand and reached for a piece of gauze to cover the site. He struggled against her.

"Mr. Crowell, listen to me," Miriam began, in a soothing voice, "I understand that you're in pain. And I want to help, but you need to calm down and lay back down in bed for me."

Haylie stood back and watched.

He whimpered. "Pills... I want a pill for pain. Can you get me something?"

"We will call the doctor right now and see if we can get you something to help you relax. And if you can do some relaxing on your own by laying down and taking some deep breaths, then I'm sure it will help relieve your pain. Can you meet me halfway and try that?"

Haylie was awed by how calm and collected Miriam was, and how she had managed to take control of the situation.

Reluctantly, Mr. Crowell sank back into bed and closed his eyes.

"Breathe with me," Miriam told him. "Long, deep breaths. In through the nose, and out through the mouth."

She worked with him until they were taking deep breaths in unison.

"Haylie," she said, calling the new nurse to the bedside. "We're going to need to start a new IV on Mr. Crowell. Can you get one for me?"

"Sure," Haylie agreed. "What gauge?"

"Twenty will be fine."

Haylie picked up an IV start kit and laid it in front of Miriam on Mr. Crowell's bed.

Miriam looked up at her. "You're his nurse, so you can start the IV," she said softly.

Haylie donned gloves and prepped the site, then inserted the needle into the best vein that she could find on his hand. Her heart was pounding as she was struggling to remember the last time that she had started an IV on an actual human being – not just a manikin or a practice arm. She thought long and hard about everything that she needed to do, and made sure not to break sterile technique.

"Okay," Miriam said softly. "Now you need to tape it down and hook up the line."

Haylie covered the needle with a square of gauze, then tore off a piece of tape and gently pressed it down over the site.

When she was done, she hooked up the line and was relieved to see the clear fluid start flowing into Mr. Crowell's vein.

"Let me show you a little trick," Miriam said. She tore another piece of tape off from Haylie's roll, and then tore a small notch at each end. She pressed that piece of tape down over the line, fitting the tubing between the notches. "It helps hold it in place," she explained to Haylie. "It's a little more comfortable for the patient, and it also makes it easier to tear off the tape when you go to remove the line."

Haylie hadn't even realized it, but she had been holding her breath throughout Miriam's demonstration. She finally let it out with a deep sigh.

Wow, was all that she could think.

Could this really be happening?

Miriam had come to her aid and had helped her get a combative patient under control. Then she watched as Haylie started an IV, and never once had anything negative to say about it. And on top of it all, she had taught Haylie something new.

Wow! Haylie thought once again. *Maybe Miriam is coming around. Maybe she's going to lighten up, and from now on, things are going to be smooth between us. Is it possible? Did it really happen that easily? Maybe she's not so horrible after all!*

"You need to give Mr. Crowell's doctor a call. Can you go take care of that, Haylie?" Miriam asked, almost sweetly.

"Sure," Haylie responded, completely in disbelief that she and her preceptor were finally engaged in a civil conversation.

At the nurse's station, she called the operator and had Dr. Perry Fox paged. It took him a little less than a minute to call in.

"Med-Surg South, this is Haylie," she said.

"It's Doc Fox. What's going on?"

"It's Mr. Crowell. He panicked and ripped out his IV earlier today and is asking for more pain medication."

There was silence at the end of the line.

"Hello?" Haylie asked.

"Is that why you called?" Dr. Fox asked sharply.

Uh oh... Haylie knew that she was in trouble, she just didn't know why. "Well, yes..."

"Don't you know the patient? He's been on your floor at least half a dozen times over the past year." He sounded agitated.

"Well... no...."

"The other nurses should have told you. He's addicted to prescription painkillers. He has to be managed very carefully with pain meds. I'm doing the most that I can for him right now."

"Okay... I'm sorry, I didn't realize..."

"Is Miriam there?" Dr. Fox asked.

"Yes. She's in there with him now."

"He responds very well to her. He's been on your floor several times before and has done the same kind of thing... has panic attacks and rips out his IV's. But Miriam can talk him down from them. All she does it sit with him for a while and walks him through deep breathing exercises, things like that. But somehow it's just enough to soothe him."

"Yes. She's doing that for him now. But she told me to call you, too."

Dr. Fox laughed softly. "Are you new?" He asked, suddenly sounding much more relaxed, much more friendly.

"Yes. Second day on the job."

He laughed again. "Go tell Miriam that Doc Fox said no more pain meds for Mr. Crowell right now, and no more making the new nurse call the doc when she knows better."

Haylie let out another deep sigh.

How dare she? She wondered. *First Miriam acts all nice to me, like she's trying to help me, and then she sends me to the phone hoping I'll get blasted by an angry doc. She totally threw me under the bus! That evil witch!*

At least Dr. Fox had been kind to her.

Isn't it supposed to be the other way around? Aren't the nurses supposed to stand together and stick up for each other, and walk on eggshells around the doctors? This just seemed all wrong.

Haylie shook her head as she returned to Mr. Crowell's room. "I called Dr. Fox," she said to Miriam.

Miriam smiled slightly. "Oh? And what kind of mood was he in today? He's normally pretty irritable this time of morning, before he's had his coffee."

Haylie narrowed her eyes and returned the smile. "He was very kind to me, actually. He said no more pain meds for Mr. Crowell. And no more of you pushing me around." *Whoa!* Haylie thought. *Did I really just say that?*

Miriam looked up at her, stunned. "He did not say that."

"Well, not in those exact words. But he sure seemed familiar enough with the situation. The new nurse getting set up to fail. He actually laughed when I said your name. That's how well he recognized what's going on here." Haylie couldn't believe that she was being this confrontational. She usually avoided conflict, but she was already sick of Miriam's antics. She felt her heart pounding as anger built within her.

Miriam stood up, nearly kicking the seat out from behind her. "Young lady, I am your preceptor and you don't talk that way to me. You've walked in here, completely incompetent, and I'm supposed to take you and make you a nurse. It's not all kittens and rainbows, you know! Some of the lessons are going to be hard. There will be times when you'll call doctors and you'll get questioned or yelled at or hung up on. Better you learn to deal with it sooner than later."

Haylie struggled to keep from raising her voice. "Of course it will happen, Miriam, I'm not stupid! I know doctors can be hard to work with. But you're actually going out of your way to make things difficult for me. Aren't you supposed to try and protect me from things like this? Aren't you supposed to prepare me for tough situations instead of throwing me into the middle of them and laughing at me while I flounder around, trying to figure out what I'm supposed to do?" Haylie felt tears come to her eyes.

Miriam stood up and walked out of the room, brushing past

Haylie. "This isn't an appropriate conversation to be having in front of a patient, and you should know better," she said. "We're done here."

Mr. Crowell was sleeping, or at least appeared to be. But Miriam was right, for once, and Haylie knew it. So she left his room and followed her to the nurse's station. "I'm not done," she said to Miriam. "We need to finish this conversation."

"No," Miriam said curtly. "We're done for now. Donna's at a meeting right now but as soon as she gets back, we can go talk with her. I want all of this documented."

"You want what documented?" Haylie asked.

"Your sour attitude and comments toward me... in front of a patient, no less..."

"He was sleeping."

"You don't know that."

Haylie gave up, realizing that she couldn't win. She went into the break room and sat down at the table, sinking her head into her hands. A few minutes later, Mel walked in.

"How goes it, new girl?" She asked cheerfully.

Haylie bit her lip, trying not to cry. "Horribly," she replied. "Miriam hates me."

Mel grinned. "No she doesn't. She's just being Miriam. You'll get used to her after a while."

Mel went to the soda machine and bought two cans of soda. She put one in front of Haylie. "Here you go. Have a drink on me."

Reaching for the soda and popping the tab, Haylie felt relief wash over her. At last... a kind gesture from a co-worker.

"I can't do anything right in her eyes," Haylie said, suddenly feeling the urge to bond with Mel and vent her frustrations. "What's the deal with her... why is she so mean?"

Mel started on her own soda. "Oh, Large Marge is who she is. Direct, a little rough around the edges, but she's a great nurse. You'll learn a lot from her. She's been doing this forever and a day."

Haylie looked at Mel curiously. "I thought we were talking about Miriam. You just said 'Large Marge'... are you talking about someone else now?"

Blushing, Mel looked away. "Oh... oops, I let that slip. Sorry. That's a little nickname we have for Miriam..."

Haylie found herself laughing. "You don't call her that to her face, do you?"

"No, of course not. Brad started it and got me hooked on it. Now I can't stop."

"So why Large Marge?"

While sipping her soda, Mel coughed slightly, as if trying not to choke. She put the can down on the table and swallowed hard, fighting giggles. "Miriam's last name is Simpson. You know... like the cartoon character..."

Haylie grinned. "Yeah. That's funny. So what's Miriam's husband's name... Homer?"

Mel doubled over in giggles. "Yeah, it is. That's why we call her Marge."

Haylie's jaw dropped. "Are you serious?"

Nodding, Mel blotted tears from her eyes. "Of course, he had that name long before the cartoon character ever came along, so he has the original claim to it. But still, you have to admit, it's funny."

"It's hysterical!" Haylie could hardly contain herself. It suddenly felt so good to be able to share a laugh with someone, even though it was tinged with a slight bit of guilt. *I know it's wrong to mock her behind her back, but who cares!* Haylie thought to herself. *She openly mocks me to my face... so she deserves it!*

"You should have been here a month ago when he was a patient on our floor," Mel began. "We were cracking up about his name the whole time. How many nurses can say that they've had Homer Simpson as a patient?"

"That is pretty funny," Haylie replied. "You and Brad seem cool. I should hang out with you sometime."

"Yeah, you should! Brad's a great guy, and a terrific nurse. You'll like him a lot once you get to know him."

Haylie nodded. "Sounds good to me. I'm just curious... how long have you guys been together?"

Mel arched her eyebrows. "What do you mean?"

"You and Brad... how long have you been together?"

Laughing, Mel shook her head. "We're not together. We're just friends. I'm almost old enough to be his mom. He's more like a little brother to me, actually."

Haylie blushed. "Oh. I'm sorry. I saw you guys in the cafeteria yesterday and I just assumed-"

"Yeah, it's okay," Mel said. "You're not alone there. We nurses try to analyze everything and everyone. We make assumptions too often. We look at our co-workers sitting down in the cafeteria together and assume they're a couple just because it's a male and a female... that kind of thing. I'm sure there are some rumors floating around about me and Brad being a couple, but trust me, we're not."

Haylie felt stupid. "My bad. I'm really sorry to assume."

Mel laughed and shrugged. "It's okay, really. We're both very much single right now. I'm a recent divorcee, and I'm way too bitter to even think about having another relationship, not for a good long while. And Brad has a girlfriend who wants him to settle down and commit, but he's not quite ready. So they just recently called it quits." Mel's eyebrows shot up a bit. "Hey, how old are you? Brad's twenty-seven you know... probably not much older than you are. And he's cute too, don't you think? Maybe you and him..."

Haylie shook her head. "Oh, no thanks. The last thing I'm interested in right now is dating anyone. All I really want to do is get comfortable with my job and be a good nurse. That's all for now."

"I can understand that," Mel replied. "But whenever you're ready, let me know and I'll talk to Brad and put in a good word for you."

"Hmmm, I'll pass, Mel, but thanks. Nothing against Brad, my mind is just occupied with a million other things right now."

"No problem. Hey... I need to get back to work. Let me know if you need help with anything, okay? And maybe we can get lunch together one day this week." She finished her soda and threw the can in the recycle bin.

"Thanks Mel. I enjoyed talking with you."

"Anytime." Mel smiled as she stepped toward the door. "Oh, and thanks for the donuts too. Listen, don't let Large Marge bring you down. She's harmless. Just ask Homer."

And suddenly, a nagging feeling settled into Haylie's gut as she recalled part of her conversation with Mel.

You should have been here a month ago when he was a patient on our floor, Mel had said.

What happened to Miriam's husband? Haylie wondered. *Surely if it had been serious, Mel would have said more about it. She probably wouldn't have spoken of it so lightheartedly in the first place.*

Right?

Returning from her nurse leadership meeting, Donna groaned as she caught bits and pieces of Mel's conversation with Haylie as she passed by the break room. It was only Haylie's second day, and already, Mel was teaching her Miriam's pet name.

Not good. Things were volatile enough already between Haylie and Miriam.

*Lord, what am I supposed to do with these nurses when they act so childishly? Help me to be a good nurse manager...*Donna prayed silently. *Because right now I'd like to just chew them out and give them all a good spanking!*

Chapter 8
Wednesday

Donna came in to work early on Wednesday morning and logged into her computer to check email.   She hadn't had a chance to check it the prior day, so she braced herself for a long list of unread messages. She started at the top of the list. Clicking on the first one made her stomach churn.

From: Simpson, Miriam R.

Re: HAYLIE

DONNA

WE HAVE TO MEET AND TALK ABOUT THIS PRECEPTOR SITUATION.   I DO NOT THINK I CAN HANDLE IT.   I HAVE SOME SERIOUS CONCERNS ABOUT HAYLIE. SHE WAS VERY INAPPROPRIATE TODAY. LET'S TALK WHEN YOU'RE BACK IN THE OFFICE.

MIRIAM

With a loud groan, Donna closed her eyes and thanked God that Haylie and Miriam were both off that day. Then she opened her eyes again and re-read Miriam's email filled with screaming capital letters. It made her stomach flip. "Why in the world is she yelling at me?" Donna wondered aloud.

Then she advanced to the next email.

From: Evans, Haylie J.

Re: Miriam

Hi Donna,

Can we please meet and talk when we're both back in the office? I am having a hard time with Miriam as my preceptor. I am trying so hard to do a good job and learn from Miriam but we are just not getting along. Is there any chance that you could assign me a new preceptor? Maybe Mel? I think she and I would work together well. Let me know what you think.

Haylie

Haylie's name was "signed" in pink script. How pretty! Donna had never seen that before in an email and wondered how Haylie had accomplished it. She looked back at Miriam's email and then at Haylie's. Such a contrast. She wondered if there was any way that she could talk Haylie into tutoring Miriam in the art of crafting and sending an email.

Then she thought about what both of the emails actually had to say, and realized how futile it would be to even try. She doubted that Miriam could fathom that she might actually be able to learn something from Haylie. And doubted even more that Haylie would want to do anything helpful for Miriam.

Donna closed her eyes, clasped her hands, and prayed hard that there would be a way to make peace between the two. Then she went back to her computer and decided to take a break from reading emails for a moment. She pulled up a blank document on her screen, and began to type a letter.

Dear Darius,

I received your letter. I love you and miss you, son, but you know how I feel about dishonesty. You and I both know that you don't need $200 to repay someone for breaking a TV set. I don't know what you really want the money for, but I don't have it to give to you right now. I'm raising your brother and sister on one income and it's all I can do to feed and clothe them. I'm sending you $20 for the canteen. I hope you'll buy another postage stamp and write to me again soon. Or call me collect. I will accept a call from you, any time ,day or night.

Right now we're waiting to hear from UNC. Sean is on the wait list so please pray that he gets in. Do you still pray, son? If not, you should. Jeannie is doing fine. She's as pretty and perfect as ever. She makes me smile every day. And so do you, whether you realize it or not. I think about you every day and I miss you. I'll always love you and be proud of you. I pray for you every day. That you will be safe and happy and healthy, and that your life will change. God has given you an opportunity to turn your life around. Will you take it, Darius? Be blessed, my boy, and come home to me soon.

Love,

Mama

Donna printed the letter on a piece of paper, which she inserted into an envelope with a $20 bill. She added the prison's address, kissed it, held it over her heart and hugged it, which was as close as she could get to hugging Darius. For a little while, anyway. She hoped that there would come a day when she could embrace her son again.

Then she went back to her computer and looked at Haylie and Miriam's emails again. *Time to take care of my other children,* she mused. *What am I going to do with these two?*

Just then – as if it were an answer to her prayers – a new email appeared in her inbox. Donna clicked the sender's name to open it.

From: Gallagher, Laura

Re: Lateral Violence Workshop Tomorrow

Dear colleagues,

Just a reminder of our continuing education workshop scheduled for Friday: "When Nurses Collide: Managing Lateral Violence" to be held 9 am to 12 noon in classroom A. All nurses are invited to attend. Please reply to this email to RSVP your attendance.

Laura Gallagher

Without thinking, Donna hit the reply button.

Laura – I'll be there on Friday, with 4 of my nurses. Wish me luck in finding coverage.

Donna

Chapter 9
Thursday

"Haylie, 2-A is ringing her call bell again," Miriam cried out from behind the desk at the nurse's station. "Go see what she wants."

Donna shook her head. "2-A? Don't you mean Mrs. Burton?"

"You know what I mean," Miriam responded. "And I'm talking to Haylie, anyway." She quickly glanced around the unit. "Haylie?" She called out. "Where is that girl?"

Haylie rounded the corner of the nursing desk. "I'm here, Miriam. I was just down the hall putting ice in Mr. Crowell's pitcher." She held up the pink pitcher and shook it to show Miriam that she had in fact been doing what she'd said she was.

Why do I have to do that? Why do I feel that I to have to justify myself to Miriam? Haylie wondered. *Oh yes... because I'm immature and incompetent.* She remembered Miriam's hurtful comments from Tuesday, and her stomach knotted with anger.

"So go take care of your patient," Miriam commanded.

"I am taking care of my patients. All of them. But I can only do one thing at a time. I'm only human, you know, I'm –"

"YOU are a nurse, young lady, human has nothing to do with it." Miriam quickly stood up and faced Haylie. "You need to exercise some common sense. Mrs. Burton is one day post-op from hip replacement surgery. There could be all kinds of things going on with her! She could be in intolerable pain, or she could be in there bleeding out all over herself. Or better yet, she could have a blood clot that ended up in her lungs and she could be in there DYING. Mr. Crowell, on the other hand is a drug-seeker –"

"Miriam –" Donna tried to interrupt her, but Miriam continued.

"He just had his third ELECTIVE back surgery, and it's the same thing every time he ends up in this unit. All he does is beg for drugs the minute he gets here and keeps on begging till the moment he leaves. There's nothing wrong with him. He's just a junkie. And YOU should have the good sense to recognize that." She snatched the pitcher out of Haylie's hands. "Now use your brain and go take care of the patient who needs you the most."

Haylie's jaw dropped. For a moment, all that she could do was blink her eyes as if she were hoping to wake up from this horrible nightmare. She couldn't even breathe.

"GO!" Miriam yelled at her, quickly snapping her out of her state of shock. She shuffled away, almost running, to Mrs. Burton's room.

Donna glared at Miriam. "That was unnecessary."

"Oh, don't start with me today," Miriam replied.

Donna took the pitcher out of Miriam's hands. "I'm going to take this ice to Mr. Crowell, and when I get back, you and me – we need to talk." She delivered the ice to Haylie's patient, and immediately returned to Miriam, pulling her into the break room and closing the door behind them.

"Miriam, you're going to kill that poor child, with your yelling and screaming. It's uncalled for."

"Oh please. She's not a child."

"No, she's not. But you certainly treat her that way. You don't talk to other adults like that..."

"Well if she'd act like an adult, maybe I'd treat her like one."

"Miriam, she's been on the job for less than a week! She's a brand new nurse. She's having to learn everything for the first time!"

"She was supposed to have learned everything in nursing school."

"But it's not the same thing as actually being a nurse. It's going to take time for her to translate what she learned in the classroom and in clinicals, and turn it into real skills. She's young, she's inexperienced, and she's overwhelmed. There's a learning curve, and you have to give her some time. And..." Donna's voice suddenly became very firm, "I want you to be nice to her. Even if it kills you. Just a little common courtesy. That's all I'm asking."

"You know what I'm going to give her? I'm going to give her my foot up her –"

The door swung opened, stopping Miriam midsentence. Haylie rushed in. "Mrs. Burton's having a weird arrhythmia, and she says she's feeling really lightheaded."

"What kind of arrhythmia?" Miriam asked, quickly shifting back into nurse mode.

Haylie's mouth opened, but no words came out. She shook her head from side to side.

Miriam's eyes narrowed. "Silly me. I can't believe I actually expected you to know the answer to that." Miriam shoved past her, her wide hips bumping against Haylie and knocking her against the wall.

"Large Marge," Haylie muttered under her breath. "Fat, evil witch... I hate her... hate her so much." She bit her lip and fought back tears.

Donna sighed loudly. "That's enough, Haylie. Mrs. Burton is still your patient, so you need to be in there with Miriam."

"Yeah, well what am I supposed to do?"

"You watch. And you learn."

***

Later in Donna's office, Haylie and Miriam sat opposite each other.

Donna rested her elbows on her desk and stared at both of them.

"Well, let's focus on the positive. Mrs. Burton is fine. You both worked together to get things under control."

"Hmmmmf," Miriam grunted. "Haylie should have been more

on top of things."

"The nurse on night shift forgot to give Mrs. Burton her heart medication. That isn't Haylie's fault." Donna defended her.

"No, it's not her fault, but she should have read the chart. She should have talked to the nurse during the change of shift." Miriam crossed her arms over her chest and glared at Haylie.

"I did talk to the nurse at change of shift. She didn't mention that she failed to give Mrs. Burton her heart medication."

"And I bet you didn't read the chart, did you?" Miriam asked.

"I didn't have time yet," Haylie said, raising her voice. "I just got here!"

Donna intervened. "But let's look at what happened. Haylie recognized that there was a problem. She wasn't sure what it was, but she sought out help from you, Miriam, and you helped her to figure out what it was. Then Haylie gave Mrs. Burton her medication, and now she's fine. So what's so horrible? Why are you two so upset?"

Miriam rolled her eyes. "She can't even identify an arrhythmia, and she's a nurse?"

"I can't do anything right in your eyes," Haylie shot back, then turned her attention to Donna. "I want to learn and I want to do a good job. I really do. It's just hard for me to do it when I'm under constant criticism."

Donna steepled her fingers and rested her chin against her thumbs, then closed her eyes as if deep in thought. "This has to stop," she said. "Do the best you can to get through today. Tomorrow, we're going to a class that I think will help all of us on the unit."

"What kind of class?" Miriam leaned forward, suddenly curious.

"It's a workshop on lateral violence," Donna replied. "It's supposed to help us think about why nurses act violently toward each other, and discover some ways to minimize it."

Taken aback, Miriam narrowed her eyes. "Violence?" She asked. "As if we were up here beating each other up?"

"Well, you are," Donna replied. "With words. And dirty looks. And not being helpful or supportive."

Haylie grinned slightly, feeling as though Miriam was the one in the hot seat. Donna noticed and quickly responded to it. "And hurtful nicknames, and talking about your co-workers behind their backs," she said, glaring at Haylie. The young nurse's smile quickly disappeared.

"Get back out on the floor, both of you. Your patients need you," Donna said.

***

Brad flipped through the channels until he found his patient's favorite TV show.

"That's it," Mr. Eldridge said, smiling with recognition as MTV's "Pimp My Ride" showed up on the screen.

Brad couldn't help but laugh out loud. "You're kidding... this is your favorite show?"

Mr. Eldridge grinned. "What, just because I'm a seventy-four year old white guy from Long Island, you think that means I can't enjoy MTV?" His thick New Englander accent was quite a departure from the normal Southern drawl that Brad was used to hearing from his patients. "You kids... you crack me up."

Brad laughed again. "Oh, I'm not a kid. I'm closer to thirty than I am twenty," he confessed.

"No kidding! Well, you sure look young," Mr. Eldridge commented. "Nothing wrong with that. I'm sure the young ladies still love ya, don't they?" He punched Brad softly on the arm and laughed loudly.

"Ehh... not really," Brad said. "Or if they do, I don't pay much attention."

"You got yourself a steady girl?" His patient asked.

Brad shrugged. "Yeah. I mean, no. I mean, I did. We kind of broke up." He turned over his name badge and showed Mr. Eldridge a tiny picture of Sue that he had taped to the back of it sometime last year.

"Wow. She's a cutie," Mr. Eldridge said. "Why in the world would you let a great gal like her get away?"

"She wants to get married and I'm not ready," Brad said sadly.

Mr. Eldridge reached for his remote control and turned down the volume on the TV. "Marriage ain't so bad, young fella. My wife, Regina and I have been together for almost fifty years. She's the best thing that's ever happened to me, ya know? Gave me two fine sons and a lifetime full of love. And she's still as gorgeous as the day I met her. She'll be around later today and every other day this week. Come back and meet her, will you?"

Brad nodded. "Of course I will. She sounds great." He left his patient's room and returned to the nurse's station, but not before he flipped over his nametag and looked at the picture of Sue for himself.

He missed her.

***

Behind the nurse's desk, Haylie hung up the phone and turned around, looking sullen.

"What's wrong?" Donna asked, with concern in her voice.

Haylie shook her head. "I just agreed to a blind date. Ugh. Could you shoot me already?"

Donna laughed. "And here you had me all worried. Looking all sour like that. I thought your best friend had died or something."

Haylie sank into a chair and crossed her arms. "If only you had been on my last blind date, you'd understand why I'm so ill. My mom and my sister keep trying to fix me up, and so far, all the guys have been complete goobers."

"Goobers," Mel laughed. "I keep telling you, Brad's cute and young and smart, and he's not a goober…"

"No, thank you," Haylie returned. "I'm not looking for cute and young and smart. I don't really want a boyfriend right now. This is all about my mom. She's all panicked that I don't have a boyfriend and she's worried that I'm not going to have a date to my sister's wedding in a few weekends. It totally stinks because now they're sending me out on all of these blind dates."

"With goobers," Mel chuckled.

Oh, it can't be all that bad," Donna wrapped an arm around

Haylie and gave her a squeeze. "You know what they say… plenty of fish in the sea. If you don't catch the right one the first time, just throw it back and keep fishing."

Miriam jumped into the conversation. "Did I hear you say something about fishing?" She smiled, looking almost human to Haylie for a change. Miriam dug into her pocket and pulled up a wallet-size picture album that was well-worn from years of being toted around and shown off to anyone that would look. She thumbed through it until she found a picture of her husband, wearing a flannel shirt, a blue baseball cap, and grinning from ear to ear. He was holding up a large wide-mouth bass. "You know, my Homer just loves to fish. Or… he *loved* to, anyway." And just like that, her smile was gone.

Haylie watched as Miriam tucked the pictures away and sighed. She wondered why Miriam kept talking about Homer like he was dead. *He was still alive, wasn't he?* She hadn't heard any differently from anyone else. She just didn't get it. Miriam had been married to Homer – a wonderful, loving man, according to everyone, including Miriam herself – for more than 30 years, yet she instantly became depressed at the mention of his name. *What was it about Homer that was so upsetting? Did Miriam really have to be so dramatic?*

"We were just talking about Haylie's love life," Donna confessed to Miriam.

Mel leaned against the counter and shrugged. "I just don't get it. I don't know why someone so young and pretty is still single. Surely someone like you has a million guys chasing after you at any given moment."

"Not really," Haylie sighed.

Miriam shook her head and laughed. "Well look around, there are PLENTY of nice young men your age working right here in this hospital."

"Like who?" Haylie asked. "And don't say Brad again," she insisted. "I don't think I want to mix work with my love life just yet. That would be too weird."

"Just trying to help," Mel interjected. "He's a good guy."

"So YOU date him," Haylie laughed.

Mel shook her head. "I've sworn off men. Didn't work out so

great the first time I tried romance and marriage and the whole nine yards, so I'm afraid I'm going to be an old maid."

Donna threw her hands up in the air in protest. "Oh please. You know you're full of it. You'll find someone new and move on someday. Your heart isn't so broken that you won't be able to let someone else love you again."

"Enough about me," Mel said with frustration. "We're trying to fix up Haylie, remember?"

"There are plenty of others, aside from Brad," Miriam said. "Like my friend Shirley's son, Dan. He's that nice-looking blonde young man that works in Emergency."

Haylie glared at Miriam. "Dan Matcher. I went to nursing school with him. Not my type."

"And why not?" Miriam demanded to know.

Suppressing a grin, Haylie looked away. "Well, he's gay."

"Oh no he's not," Miriam shot back at her. "I'm friends with his mother. I'm sure she would have told me if he was gay." She rolled her eyes. "See Haylie, you're just making excuses. No reason why you can't go talk to him and get to know him better. Go have lunch with him someday. He's always eating around one o'clock with his roommate, Eric – that cute little fellow from Medical Records. See… there's another possibility for you. Both Dan and Eric. They're such nice, handsome young men."

The room suddenly cleared. Mel ran into the break room, faking a coughing fit to cover her laughter, and Donna quickly jetted away into one of her patient's rooms with her hand cupped over her mouth and tears spilling down her cheeks.

Haylie arched one eyebrow. "Please tell me you're kidding. Miriam. They're gay. As in… boyfriends… to each other. They're not interested in women."

Miriam's face burned crimson red. "You're assuming that. Just because they live together and eat lunch together doesn't make them gay. But I guess you just know everything, don't you? Here I go again, trying to help you out, but you don't want my help. No, you're just so smart, I couldn't possibly know what I'm talking about." Her tone was much more nasty and bitter than usual.

Haylie was taken aback. "There's no need to get defensive, Miriam."

"Of course not. You whine and complain to Donna about what a witch I am, but when I try to be nice to you, you throw it back in my face. Do me a favor – the next time you need someone to come in and clean up the messes you make with your patients… don't call me." Miriam gave her a dirty look, then shook her head and shuffled away, mumbling something under her breath.

Haylie's vision blurred, and she felt tears spilling down her own cheeks. *Oh no you don't,* she scolded herself. *Get a grip. Do NOT cry at work. Do NOT cry over witchy old Miriam, she's not worth the tears. Don't cry. DO NOT CRY!*

But she couldn't help it.

Haylie covered her face and ran to the bathroom, locking the door behind her, shutting out everyone and everything on the unit. She sat down on the floor and wept for a long, long time.

And when she was done, she happened to glance up at a piece of paper taped to the back of the door. It was a poster from the infection control department, with a picture of a grinning devil on it, complete with horns and a pitchfork. The caption read: "You don't know what the devil is on your hands, so wash them!"

Haylie stood up and reached into her pocket for her ink pen. She crossed out the infection control poster's caption, and wrote one word over the devil to replace it:

MIRIAM.

***

It didn't take long for Miriam to venture into the bathroom and promptly step right back out, her face crimson red again.

"Enough!" She cried. "Donna, this has gone far enough!"

Donna stepped out of a patient's room and waved Miriam into her office. "What now?" She asked with dread.

Miriam threw the poster onto her desk. "Look at what that little brat did. Can you believe it? This is definitely her handwriting, and she just walked out of the bathroom before I walked in."

Donna couldn't help it. She laughed. "Sorry," she apologized. "But you have to admit, Miriam, you've been pretty mean to her. It's inappropriate, yes, and I will address it with her, but I'm also not surprised. A person can only take so much ..."

"So much what?"

"Bullying," Donna replied, without missing a beat. "You're bullying her. I've seen you come down hard on some new grads before, but I've never seen you quite so harsh as the way you're acting with Haylie. What's going on with you, Miriam?"

Sinking into a chair in front of Donna's desk, she moaned loudly. "I don't know, Donna. Okay... I admit, I've been really hard on her. But she frustrates me... she walks in here like an immature airhead, with her bubbly attitude and her donuts and her cute little tattoos..."

"Only one tattoo that you know of. Which is very well covered up. You notice she went and bought new scrubs?"

"Yeah, I did."

"And the donuts... you know what that was all about, don't you? She was just trying to smooth things over with you. And maybe make some friends up here."

Miriam shook her head. "Well, she should know she can't buy us with a box of donuts."

"She's not trying to buy us. Quit being so dramatic. The poor girl just wants to be accepted and fit in. Would it really be so hard to lighten up on her? Just a little bit?"

Miriam shrugged. "I'll try. As long as you don't let her get off the hook for writing my name on the picture of the devil."

Resisting the urge to grin, Donna nodded. "As I said, I'll address it with Haylie."

"Thank you." Miriam rose to leave.

"Hey Miriam," Donna called out to her as she was leaving her office, "Is everything okay at home? How are you coping?"

"Just fine, everything's fine," Miriam said, a little too quickly.

***

Miriam was still surprised at times by how quiet it was in the house when she got home from work. Like no one was home.

She walked into the bedroom and changed out of her scrubs into her fleece housecoat, and threw her bulky nametag – with all of the code cards and quick reference guides attached to it – onto her nightstand.

It had been a long day, and Haylie, the world's greenest young nurse, had gotten on her last nerve. Too bad they didn't teach things like common sense and courtesy and respect in nursing school, because this poor girl just had none of her own. Miriam couldn't remember a time when she'd had to work with someone so stupid and immature. She felt her blood pressure rising again, and she sat down on the edge of the bed, taking deep breaths to relieve her stress. Sensing that it wasn't working, she reached for her bottle of blood pressure pills. Miriam sighed softly to herself. *I can't let Homer see me like this, all red-faced and angry. I've got to be strong for him.*

After a few more deep breaths, she stood up and walked into the spare bedroom of the house, which she and Homer had turned into a library after their son grew up and left home. It had gorgeous French windows that let a lot of sunlight into the room, so it was always warm and bright; the perfect spot to sit and read for a while. There were three bookshelves stacked with old copies of Readers' Digest, Alfred Hitchcock books, Homer's hunting and fishing magazines, and all the other books and magazines that they had accumulated during the years.

And even though Homer didn't read much anymore, he still liked this room in the house the best. He would sometimes sit for hours in front of the windows, basking in the sunlight.

Miriam stepped behind Homer, clearing her throat to let him know that she was there and not startle him. She reached down to where he sat in his wheelchair, wrapping her arms around his shoulders, and giving him a kiss on his cheek. The right side, of course, the one that still had feeling in it.

"Ah fought ah hur you come ih."

I thought I heard you come in, Homer said.

It had taken some time to learn how to decipher Homer's speech after the massive stroke that he'd had a month ago, but Miriam was now fluent in Homer-ish.

"Was ih a gooh gay ah wuhk?"

Was it a good day at work?

"Of course it was, Homey. Everything was great."

"You wyah."

You liar.

"Really, Homeybear, everything is okay. It was a very good day."

He shook his head. "Yo faif ih hot. You upthet."

Your face is hot. You're upset.

Darn if Homer didn't know her better than anyone else in the world.

"Don't worry about me. I promise everything is fine."

"Ith not. I am stih hee fo yo."

"What?"

"I... I....am stih hee. Don ack ligh I deah. Nah yeh."

"Homey, I don't understand."

He banged his fist down on the armrest of his wheelchair.

"Awww," Homer let out an exasperated sigh. "Thit."

Miriam gasped. "I understood *that*," she said. "And as I've told you before, I'll have none of that foul language in my house."

He groaned in protest.

"Don't worry, Homey," Miriam hugged him more tightly. "I just want you to get... better, before you go worrying about me and all."

"I not gon to geh behh."

I'm not going to get better.

Miriam fought back tears. "Don't say that. Yes you are."

"I not. You haf to accef tis."

I'm not. You have to accept this. Homer was right. His doctor had agreed to as much. After his first stroke two years ago, he had recovered fairly well. But this one had done more massive damage, and Miriam had been warned that the next one would be the last.

"I'm sorry, dear. I'm not understanding you again." But the truth was, she'd understood exactly what Homer had been saying to her all along.

I am still here for you.   I am still here.   Don't act like I am dead. Not yet.

Miriam had gone about her life in a comfortable state of denial. What did the doctor know, anyway? There was no guarantee that Homer would have another stroke at some point, just because he'd already had two. And who was to say that Homer wouldn't fully recover from this latest one, just like he did from the first one?

"Thit," said Homer.

And tears came to Miriam's eyes. As offensive as she found such language, she wished she could hear Homer say the real word again. Even if only once more, it would be music to her ears.

Chapter 10
Friday

"Please sign the roster as you walk in. There's some coffee and some bagels in the back of the room. Find a seat and we'll be getting started right at nine o'clock." The trainer paced back in forth at the front of the room, her curly brown hair bouncing across her shoulders with each turn on her heel. She cast a shadow on the white screen each time she stepped in the path of the LCD projector.

There were probably twenty or so other nurses in the room already. Haylie recognized some familiar faces from having passed them in the hallways or in the cafeteria. At a glance, though, she was fairly certain that she was the youngest one in the room. That always made her feel awkward. She hoped that the trainer didn't put her on the spot and make her answer questions that she didn't know the answers to. How horrible that would be, to suffer embarrassment like that in front of her co-workers, all of whom had been in the workforce longer and were more experienced.

She sat down at a table between Donna and Mel and looked at the handout in front of her. The cover page, which was fluorescent pink, practically yelled out the title of the workshop and the name of the trainer:

"When Nurses Collide: Managing Lateral Violence"

Laura Gallagher, MSN, RN

Underneath the words was a picture of two cartoon nurses – with really small bodies and huge heads – in bumper cars, smashing into each other. She nudged Mel and Donna and pointed to the picture with her pencil. "Look," she said, "It's me and Miriam."

"It sure is," Donna said.

Mel nodded and showed her agreement by writing Miriam and Haylie's names over the pictures of the nurses on her own handout.

Miriam and Brad, with coffee and bagels in hand, sat down at the table behind the three of them. Haylie blushed and hoped that Miriam hadn't overheard her comment. But then again, if she had, how could she argue with her? They'd had their fair share of collisions, that was for sure. No bumper cars required.

"Let's get started," the trainer said in a loud voice. "Welcome. My name is Laura and I'm happy to be here with you today. I know that you all have busy schedules and that it's asking a lot for you to give up a few hours of work to be here. So, I really want to be respectful of your time and make sure that this day is meaningful for you. The first thing I'd like to do is meet each of you, and find out what it is that you'd like to get from this program. So let's go around the room. Please introduce yourself, and tell me a little bit about you... like how long you've been working as a nurse, or maybe something you do to relieve stress after a hard day at work... and then tell me what you hope to learn today."

Laura pointed to the first person in the front row, and started off the introductions. She wrote each person's name on a flip chart at the front of the room, and made notes next to each person.

After the introductions were done, Laura asked everyone to look at the flip chart. "Look at what a diverse group we have here," she said. "We have people who have more than thirty years of experience in nursing," she said, referring specifically to Miriam, "and then we have people with only a few days worth of experience," which of course, meant Haylie, "and everything in between."

Haylie could just imagine Miriam smiling smugly behind her.

"But having a diverse group is a great thing," Laura continued, "because we'll get lots of different perspectives and reactions to what we're going to talk about today. So let's get started. How many of you are familiar with the term 'lateral violence'.... Anyone?"

A few hands hesitantly raised up around the room. Donna's was one of them, so Laura pointed to her.

"Donna," she said, "Would you mind sharing with us what lateral violence is?"

Nodding, Donna put her hand back down on the table. "It's when nurses eat their young – and each other," she said. The rest of the class reacted with laughter.

Laura smiled. "Interesting you'd put it that way," she said. "Where does that term 'eat their young' come from?"

"From nature," Donna replied. "Some species of animals do it. Lions, tigers, baboons and other species of animals have been observed cannibalizing their own offspring. And even sometimes each other."

The trainer crossed her arms and looked around the room as if deep in thought. "And is that what nurses do? Are we cannibals too?"

"Sometimes," Haylie blurted out, without thinking. She instantly felt embarrassed and felt her face begin to blush. She heard Miriam grunt behind her. "I mean, not literally, but yes. Nurses tear each other down sometimes."

Laura shrugged. "What do the rest of you think?"

There was a moment of silence.

"Yes," responded a soft voice at the back of the room.

"Yeah," said another nurse, closer to the front of the room.

"I think so." Another one.

"Right. Yeah." Brad chimed in.

Donna and Mel didn't speak aloud, but both were nodding.

"So why do animals eat their young?" Laura asked.

"For survival of the species," Miriam said, without missing a beat. "If their young – or others in their pack – aren't strong enough or fast enough or skilled enough, then they'll ultimately bring the rest of the pack down."

Laura looked around the classroom for the reaction. "And what about nurses?"

"The same reason," Miriam responded. "Some people aren't meant to be nurses. They're not competent enough to do the job.

So they need to know that they're not cut out for it, and they need to get out."

"So the pack turns on them to let them know?" Laura offered.

Miriam nodded. "Basically, yes."

"Okay," Laura continued. "Does anyone feel differently? Does anybody think that there could be another reason why nurses act violently toward each other?"

A younger nurse - with just a few months more work experience than Haylie – took a deep breath from the back of the room. "I think it's because the older nurses that I work with are jealous of me." There were audible grunts of disagreement throughout the room, and everyone turned to look at the young woman as she continued to speak. "I'm younger, I'm happier, I'm prettier, I'm in better shape. I'm not coming to work complaining of marriage problems and lazy children and bad knees and migraines and bills I can't pay."

The mood in the room became tense, as people crossed their arms and rolled their eyes. All except for Haylie, who suddenly had the urge to pick up her handout and run to the back of the room and hug the nurse who had just spoken.

"Or maybe," Miriam blurted out, "The 'older' nurses are just frustrated with the newer ones." She put special emphasis on the word 'older' to make the point that the label offended her. "Maybe it's just hard for the nurses who have been here longer to keep taking new nurses under their wings and teach them things over again, day in and day out, things that they should have learned in nursing school, but apparently didn't."

"Well frankly, I think there's more to it than just what's going on at work," Donna offered. "I think we all come to work with our own stress from our personal lives. Anybody who knows me knows that I have three babies – mostly all grown up – but they're still my babies. One, I'm trying to get into college. One, I'm just hoping will make it out of prison one day and get himself back on his feet. And one is in ninth grade and spends most of her time dreaming about ways to get rich and famous, thinking it will solve all of our family's problems. And I'm a widow. I've got no partner to get me through the rest of my life, and my children have no father anymore. That's a lot on my shoulders. And I can't just pack it all up and put it away for twelve hours at a time when I come to work every day. It's still a part of me."

Donna had a good point. Haylie thought quietly about what all of her other co-workers were dealing with. Miriam had a husband who apparently had experienced some recent health problems and a hospitalization. Mel was still coping with a bitter divorce, and Brad had his on-again, off-again relationship with Sue.

And Haylie thought about her own life and how she just wanted everyone to let her be who she was. Her mother wanted her to marry young and start making babies, her friends wanted her to stay young and party all the time, and her co-workers – Miriam in particular – expected her to be the perfect nurse. She sometimes felt as if she was trapped in a room in which the walls were closing in. So much pressure, from every angle, and it seemed at times that she just couldn't make anyone happy, let alone herself. And like Donna said, she couldn't just pack it up and put it away for twelve hours at a time, each day that she had to go in to work. All of that stress was still there.

Laura smiled as she spoke. "You all are making some really interesting points," she said. She pointed her remote mouse to the screen at the front of the room, clicked it once to wake the computer up from sleep mode, and her slideshow appeared.

The first slide read:

Q: What is Lateral Violence?

A: Any culture that has been oppressed will inevitably turn on itself.

Arlene Delaronde – Mohawk woman from Kahnawake, Quebec

There was quiet throughout the room for at least a full minute.

A middle-aged male nurse broke the silence. "What does that quote mean by "oppressed?"

"Think about it," Laura asked. "Think about other groups throughout history – around the world and in different cultures - that have been oppressed."

"I can think of plenty," the male nurse replied, "the Jews during the Holocaust. African slaves in early America. Even Native American Indians, like the woman you quoted. But how are we oppressed as nurses?"

Laura advanced to the next slide, which read:

Causes of lateral violence:

- *Nurses generally don't have sufficient control over their work environment*
- *High degree of accountability coupled with low degree of autonomy*
- *Workloads at unsustainable levels*

"That's all true," Donna said. Waves of "mmm-hmmm's" and nodding heads rippled throughout the room.

"But why?" Asked the nurse who had walked in a few minutes late and had taken her seat next to Haylie. She had written "Adriane" on her nametag.

"Oh, I can tell you why," Mel said, craning her neck to look at the latecomer. "You just walked in five minutes late, right? I bet anything I know the reason behind it. A doc held you up, didn't he?"

Looking down at Mel, the latecomer nurse arched her eyebrows. "As a matter of fact, yes, he did."

"Well there you go," Mel replied, turning her attention back to Laura. "Low autonomy. The docs come around for five minutes at a time, bark out orders, throw the occasional temper tantrum, and we have to stand by and be polite and agreeable and do whatever they say for the rest of the eleven hours and fifty five minutes that they're not there."

"Ah," Laura commented, her smile growing. "Let's talk more about that. When Mel was asking Adriane why she was late, she instantly attributed it to a doctor – who she assumed was a male. Her exact words were 'A doc held you up, didn't *he*?' Am I right Mel?"

Nodding in response, Mel glanced at Adriane. "Most of the docs I work with here are male. By a huge majority. And I just assumed it would be the same for you."

Adriane nodded in her direction.

"And you're right," Laura replied. "For now, anyway. Physician demographics are changing. More women are coming into practice, but it's a slow-occuring change. Medicine is very much a male-dominated profession right now, and will be for several years to come."

"And nursing is the opposite," Adriane chimed in. "Most of us are women. And that's not changing quite as quickly."

Brad threw his hands up defensively. "Okay... if you all are going to turn this into a male-bashing session, tell me now so I can get out of here and go back to work."

Laura approached Brad and shook her head. "No male-bashing," she said. "That certainly wouldn't be constructive or helpful. I don't want anyone in here to feel uncomfortable – male or female, but there is a valid point to what Mel and Adriane are talking about. Historically, nursing evolved into a profession during a time when there weren't many places for women in the workplace. And even then, nursing wasn't fully recognized as a career for quite some time. Nurses weren't seen as professionals, they were seen as handmaidens. Servants to physicians – mostly male physicians. Do you think that nurses are still seen that way?"

Most of the class either nodded or verbalized an affirmative response.

"Who were the first nurses?" Laura asked.

"Oh, I know this one," Haylie said with excitement. "We talked about this on the first day of nursing school. They were prostitutes. Like during the civil war, when soldiers ended up getting sick and wounded, there weren't enough other soldiers to take care of them. So they went looking for help among the... locals, I guess you'd say. Brothels became hospitals, and prostitutes became nurses."

"Exactly," Laura said. "Prostitutes were the very first nurses. Think about the social standing of prostitutes. What did people think of them?"

"People thought poorly of them, of course," offered Donna. "That's why they called brothels 'houses of ill repute.' Because of the bad reputation."

"So from the very beginning," Laura resumed, "the women taking care of the sick and wounded were seen as a lower class of people."

"Right. They were just servants to men," said Mel. "In more ways than one."

A few people in the class laughed softly.

"But there's a reason why they were seen that way," Miriam said, a bit angrily. "They were PROSTITUTES. They were doing something immoral and illegal for a living. They didn't have any training or skills to take care of sick people. They became nurses by default, just because there was no one else around to do it."

"You're right," Laura agreed. "Nursing as a profession certainly has come a long way since its beginnings, hasn't it? But think about what still remains. That initial image, that mindset – that nurses are, as Mel said, servants."

Laura watched as heads nodded around the room.

"You're right," said Adriane. "Servants, who are much less important than doctors. "Not as smart, not as skilled, not as competent. We're just servants that carry out orders."

Laura arched an eyebrow. "So all of you in here – trained, credentialed professionals, who work long, twelve and sixteen-hour shifts, and provide, by far, most of the hands-on care that your patients receive – would you agree that you're still primarily seen as servants to the doctor, correct?"

More nods and yeses.

"By whom?" Laura asked the question.

"By our patients," Mel offered.

"And the doctors, too," Miriam said.

"By ourselves," Adriane said softly. "We're even guilty of seeing ourselves that way. I was too scared to interrupt Dr. Soto and tell him that I had to come to class today, so that's why I was late."

Laura cocked her head. "You were scared? Of a doctor?"

"Of course I was!" Adriane replied.

"Why? Is he your boss? Do you report to him? Does he complete your performance evaluation?"

Adriane shook her head with each inquiry. "No, on all counts."

"But you still recognize him as an authority over you?"

"Yes I do. He's a doctor."

"With no real power over you. Just perceived power."

Adriane seemed to grow frustrated. "Of course he has power over me. He has the power to make my life a living hell! I called him once in the middle of the night because he had a patient who was going downhill, and he yelled at me because I woke him up! We're supposed to call the docs if that happens, and they're supposed to come in, whether it's in the middle of the day or middle of the night. That's their job! But he yelled at me over the phone, hung up on me and had me in tears. I didn't know if he was even going to come in or not and the patient was in really bad shape." Adriane's eyes began to mist at just the memory of the experience.

Laura paused for a minute. "Do you think that was acceptable behavior on his part?"

"Of course not," Adriane said. Haylie handed her a napkin and she blotted her eyes dry.

"So what did you do – confront him about it? File a complaint?"

"No way," Adriane replied.

Laura stepped closer toward her. "And why not?" The conversation took on the air of a courtroom trial, with Adriane on the stand as a witness.

"Because he's a doctor," she said. "You just don't do that."

"Because he's a doctor," Laura echoed. She paused for effect. "As if the rules don't apply to him. As if he has the right to treat you that way. As if he were some kind of god."

Miriam shifted uncomfortably in her seat. "Well they are gods around here," she said. "They get the best parking places, they've got their own private lounges, they even get free coffee in the cafeteria. They make easily four to five times what we do, and we have to pay for our stinking coffee! Don't get me wrong, there are some wonderful, smart docs here, and I know how hard they work. In a lot of ways they really do deserve those rewards... but what about us? What about nurses? Are we any less important?"

The entire room was nodding in agreement with Miriam. Even Haylie, who was surprised to hear such a cry of frustration from someone who she had seen as so powerful.

Laura nodded. "So I think we all agree that there's still quite a bit of oppression among nurses."

More nods, more yeses.

"And just to be clear, we're not bashing males, and not bashing doctors. We're just talking about a cultural phenomenon that has been observed frequently throughout history, and all around the world, which has manifested itself in modern day nursing. A culture that has been oppressed will inevitably turn on itself." She advanced to the next slide:

What is Violence?

- *Violence occurs when anyone harms, or threatens to harm a person's body, feelings or possessions*
- *Violence is a learned behavior*
- *Violence comes from within our own community (horizontal or lateral)*
- *Violence leaves victims to deal with fallout*

Miriam squinted as she read the slides. "That makes it sound like we're stabbing and shooting each other up on the unit all day," she commented. Everyone laughed, including Laura.

"I certainly hope not," Laura responded. "Violence among nurses usually isn't physical. It rarely is in groups that are mostly women." She clicked the remote mouse, bringing up the next slide:

*Lateral Violence "Top Ten" Among Nurses:**

1. *Infighting*
2. *Backstabbing*
3. *Broken confidence*
4. *Failure to respect privacy*
5. *Scapegoating*
6. *Non-verbal innuendo*
7. *Verbal affront*
8. *Undermining activities*
9. *Sabotage*
10. *Withholding information*

Heads began to nod around the room. Haylie read the list and looked up at Laura. *Oh, so I see you've worked with Miriam before*, she resisted the urge to say.

---

*Griffin, M. (2004). Teaching cognitive rehearsal as a shield for lateral violence: An intervention for newly licensed nurses. *The Journal of Continuing Education in Nursing*, 35(6), 257-263. Used with permission.

"So while there may not be shootings and stabbings on your unit, do you ever see any of these things happening?" Laura glanced around the room and could almost see light bulbs illuminating over the heads of the audience members.

Lots of nodding heads.

"Have any of you been the victims of any of these types of violence? If you think you have been, please stand up and come to the front of the room."

Without hesitation, everyone in the room pushed back their chairs, stood up and lined the wall at the front of the room.

"Thanks. You can sit down. Now the tougher question – have any of you actually done any of these things to a fellow nurse?"

Not surprisingly, no one stood up.

Again, Haylie had to resist the urge to open her mouth. Where was Rod Roddy when you needed him? She would have given anything in that moment to have heard "The Price is Right" theme song come piping into the classroom, right after he cried out "*Miriam Simpson, come on down!*"

But, Miriam did not stand up. No one did. The class attendees began to look around the room, and it began to grow uncomfortable. Until at last, Donna stood up.

Donna? Haylie was taken aback for the second time that day. *How could the motherly, kind, wise Donna possibly have ever been violent toward anyone else in her life?*

When Donna reached the front of the room, Laura placed her hand on her shoulder. "These behaviors are so ingrained in the culture of nursing that we don't even recognize when we're doing them ourselves." Then she turned her attention to Donna. "You should be proud of yourself," she told her. "So far, you're the only honest person in this room."

"Well, I'm not proud of what I've done to other nurses before," she said. "And I would have never thought of myself as a 'violent' person, but when I looked at that list, I realized that, indeed, I'm guilty as charged."

Laura nodded. "Is there a story you'd feel comfortable sharing?"

Donna looked down at the floor and closed her eyes for a

moment, deep in thought. "Yes," she said. "Well, I'm not perfect, and I could give you a long list of times I've behaved badly. But there is one thing that I've always felt bad about, more than anything else. So I guess now is as good a time as any to get it off my chest." She shifted from foot to foot and swallowed hard.

"Take your time," Laura coaxed her.

Donna began. "At the last hospital where I worked, I was a nurse manager on a med-surg unit, very similar to the one that I'm on now. And I worked with a great nurse named Cathy. She was smart and kind, and a really hard worker. Well, one day she came to me and asked me to nominate her for one of the hospital's service excellence awards. I told her I would. I filled out the form and wrote up a nice narrative for her, and even gave her a copy. But I didn't send it in."

Haylie felt as if her jaw would hit the floor. Out of the corner of her eye, she saw Mel's eyebrows shoot up on her forehead in an expression of complete shock.

"I didn't send it in," Donna continued, "because I didn't want her to get the award. I wanted the award for myself. No one had ever thought enough of me to nominate me for it, and you weren't allowed to nominate yourself, so I wasn't about to let Cathy get it. I deserved it every bit as much as her, if not more."

Laura nodded. "You weren't going to lift her up when no one was willing to do that for you."

Donna nodded shamefully. "And she was devastated when she didn't get it. She would have gotten a raise and everything. She really needed that money. She was a single mom with two kids."

Laura patted her shoulder. "Thanks for sharing that story, Donna. You can sit back down now." Donna took her seat.

An older nurse in the back of the room made a comment without any prompting. "That's number nine on the list. Sabotage."

"Good observation," Laura commented. "Sometimes sabotage can be very blatant, like setting someone up to fail in a very damaging way. And sometimes it can be passive, like in this case. But the important thing to look at here is why it happened."

Mel spoke up. "I think I understand. Donna didn't send in the award nomination form because she felt powerless. She needed recognition for a job well done and there was no one there to give it to her, so she withheld the same thing from someone else. The only power that she had in that situation was the power to keep Cathy from advancing, so that's what she did."

Crossing the room to where Mel sat, Laura nodded in her direction. "Good," she said, "you get it. That's what internalized oppression is. It's about exercising power toward someone in either a similar or weaker position than you, in the interests of protecting yourself."

"Like I said, survival of the species," Miriam piped in.

"Or so we may fool ourselves into thinking," Laura remarked. "Once we eat all of our young – and the other nurses around us – who is left? Has anyone heard about the nursing shortage in America these days?" Laura asked, with a hint of sarcasm.

The audience responded with laughter. "It's not really all that funny when you think about it," she said. "When nurses are asked why they leave their jobs, nursing culture consistently comes up as one of the primary reasons reported. Lateral violence is a big part of that culture."

The older male nurse from the back of the room piped in. "We had three new nurses quit just within the past few months," he began. "And I almost didn't get to come to this class today because we're so short staffed. We've got agency nurses on the floor right now. I sure wish I could turn back the hands of time and figure out whatever it was that made those three new people leave, and then do whatever it took to get them back. 'Cause frankly it's scaring me to hear all this."

Laura nodded. "What is it you're scared of?"

"I'm scared to death of there not being anyone to take care of me when the day comes that I'm the patient," he said.

And with that comment, a hush fell upon the room.

Laura looked at her watch. "This feels like a good stopping point. Let's take a break," she said. "See you all back in fifteen minutes."

***

After the break, the five nurses from Med-Surg South filed back into the classroom and took their seats. Haylie looked around the room, reading the nametags of the individuals who had been notable commentators in the morning's discussion.

The older male nurse in the back of the room was named Bill. The younger nurse who had irritated a lot of the "older" nurses with her comments was named Gena. Another nurse in the back of the room who had been quite vocal that morning was Vicky. Haylie recognized her voice as she finished up a cell phone conversation and sat down in her seat.

Laura welcomed everyone back to the class and instructed them to look in their handouts for a worksheet titled "Managing Lateral Violence." Everyone flipped to the correct page and raised up their pens and pencils, as several rows of blank lines cued them in that a writing exercise would follow.

"Let's go back to the top ten list," Laura started. "The first item on the list is infighting. Can someone explain what that means?"

Brad was happy to volunteer. "Cat fighting... MEOW!" he responded. Everyone in the class laughed as he continued. "It's when people – your peers, I guess – start bickering with each other."

"Right," Laura said. "And what we want to do with each of the top ten is look at some responses or interventions. Things that we can say or do to stop violent behavior and keep it from escalating. So since infighting is the first one, what is it we can do when we find ourselves involved in a 'cat fight' as Brad put it?"

"I think the most important thing to do is just plain stop," Donna said. "When people start fighting, their emotions are all riled up, they're not thinking clearly, and that's never a good thing, especially when you're around patients."

"Good," Laura praised her. "Sometimes though, when you're in the middle of a heated argument, you may need a verbal cue to stop the fight. So what's a phrase you could use to stop an argument?"

"Let's stop fighting," said Donna. "Or maybe something like 'this isn't the time or the place. We need to discuss this later,' That might work."

Laura nodded. "Super. And what do you do if the person doesn't respond to that? What if he or she insists on continuing the fight?"

"Then you should walk away," said Bill, from the back of the room. "It takes two to fight, and if you just remove yourself from the situation – don't worry about winning or having the last word – then you're taking control just by leaving."

Everyone in the class started making notes on their paper as Laura gave Bill a thumbs-up sign.

"Next one – backstabbing." Laura said. "This is a big one. What's the remedy?"

"Stab in the front instead of the back," Brad offered, making everyone laugh again.

"Well, that's one way of putting it," the trainer agreed with a laugh. "We have to monitor our own behavior and not talk about others when they're not around. But what do you do if someone comes to you and wants to talk about someone else behind their back?"

Haylie decided to jump in. "You can refuse to participate in the backstabbing. Just don't comment back."

"Or even better," said Adriane, "you can say something like 'I don't feel comfortable talking about her while she's not here. If you have a problem with her, you should probably go talk to her directly, anyway.'"

Laura walked over to where Haylie and Adriane sat and high-fived both of them. "Awesome," she said. "You've got it. You guys are making this too easy for me! I bet you're going to ace this one, too – broken confidences. Let's say that your co-worker, Jane Doe, tells you that she's thinking of resigning, but asks you to keep it between the two of you. Then your manager comes along and tells you that she's heard a rumor that Jane might be resigning, and wants to know if you've heard anything. How do you handle that?"

Vicky took this one. "Well... if someone told you something in confidence, you don't break it, simple as that. It's hard to work together if you can't trust each other. And if someone starts hitting you up for the information, you just have to flat out tell them – I was asked to keep that confidential. If you want to know if Jane's resigning, then go ask her."

Laura nodded. "And if you hear someone else breaking a confidence?"

"Then you can still speak up," Vicky suggested. "Just say something like 'that sounds to me like something that should be confidential.' You can at least try to protect whatever was said in confidence."

"Excellent," Laura said, nodding enthusiastically. "Now here's a tough one… failure to respect privacy."

Haylie put her pen down and looked up, glancing around the class. She was interested in hearing what her co-workers had to say about this one. After the multiple unwanted efforts of Mel to match her and Brad up, and Miriam's snarky comments about her tattoo, both to her face and behind her back, she felt like her privacy had been violated enough. When none of them spoke, she collected her thoughts for a moment and made a comment.

"I think it's important to draw the line between a person's personal life and their work life. Like who I date and whether or not I have a tattoo. That's my personal business. It has absolutely nothing to do with my job. And if I tell my co-workers that I don't want to discuss it, or have it discussed behind my back, then they should respect that. And if they try to talk about it while I'm around, I guess I just need to tell them – that's my private life, I don't want to discuss it here at work."

Laura nodded. "Good point – thanks, Haylie."

Miriam cleared her throat. "Well now wait a minute," she began. "Something like a tattoo could very well affect your work performance. If it's in a place where patients can see it, and they're offended by it…"

"Then that's an issue that the manager needs to deal with," Donna said sharply to Miriam, giving her a dirty look over her shoulder.

"I agree with you, Donna," Laura said. "We all have a right to our privacy and our personal lives, and we're not obligated to share everything with our co-workers about ourselves. You have to speak up when you feel that your privacy is being violated, and tell your colleagues that you don't want to discuss or share whatever it is that's being talked about. And to take it a step further, there may be times when you observe the privacy of others being violated. What do you do then?"

Gena spoke up from the back of the room. "Two nurses on my unit were talking the other day about one of the night shift nurses. They were saying that they smelled alcohol on her breath when they got to work that morning and they think she has a drinking problem. I overhead it – and I didn't jump in and gossip with them – but I guess I could have made a comment. Like 'I don't think you should be discussing this while she's not here'… would that be appropriate?"

Laura nodded. "That's a pretty serious thing that they were talking about, and if it's a legitimate concern, it should have been discussed privately with a manager, not a peer. That's how rumors get started and create a hostile work environment, and trust is completely eroded in the people you work with. But there are other times too, when gossip is just plain gossip and it doesn't need to continue. Let's say that Brad walks in on me and Donna, talking about Haylie's tattoo or her boyfriend, just hypothetically speaking. We all know that Haylie likes to keep those things private, then he can just simply say, 'It bothers me to talk about this without Haylie's permission.' And it puts the burden on me and Donna to find something else to talk about."

Everyone scribbled notes on their handouts.

Bill spoke up from the back of the room. "I'm starting to get it," he said. "It's not enough just to refrain from doing the top ten big 'no-no's' yourself. And it's not enough to just not participate when others are doing them. You're saying that we should take an active role in putting a stop to them, right? We should start speaking up and confronting these behaviors as they happen, and start letting our co-workers know that we don't find them acceptable."

Laura, in an excited rush, ran to the front of the room and faced her audience. "You're exactly right. Oppression feeds off of passivity. Speaking up is what it takes to change the culture. After enough people start voicing their discontent with the top ten lateral violence behaviors, and they keep doing it for long enough, then it's no longer easy, safe – or even practical for that matter – for people to continue those behaviors."

Bill smiled, proud to be the teacher's pet.

"Let's take on another one," Laura said. "Scapegoating. One person gets blamed for all the problems. Haylie, how do you handle it when you walk into the break room and everyone's complaining about me? Saying that I've screwed up everything?"

Haylie thought for a minute. "Well, I don't think that one person could possibly be the cause of every single problem on our unit. But what could I say to get that point across?"

"Say just that," said Laura. "That would work. Or something like

'I don't think that's the right connection.' And encourage the people who have a problem with me to discuss it with me directly."

Haylie nodded, making notes. "Got it."

"We're on a roll now," Laura continued, "and we're at my most favorite number in the big ten. Number six... non-verbal innuendo."

Everyone in the class looked around the room at each other. Some were smiling, some were groaning, others were shaking their heads.

"What a Pandora's box, huh?" asked Laura with a laugh. "The cure for non-verbal communication is pretty easy, though – verbal communication. Say something like, 'it looks like there's more you want to say to me. It's okay to speak to me directly.' Then you're giving the person the responsibility to respond to you verbally."

"Does that actually work?" Asked Haylie.

"You try it and tell me," Laura suggested. "You'll have plenty of opportunities, I'm sure. Eighty percent of all communication is non-verbal. And a lot of it in nursing units is violent-natured too. Can you all throw out a few examples?"

"Rolling eyes," volunteered Gena. "I hate that."

"Oh, and don't forget, the disapproving head shake," Adriane quickly followed.

Donna threw up her hands with excitement. "Oooh, I got one," she said. "And this isn't even so much about the people I work with. It's what my kids do to me all the time, and it drives me crazy. They don't even look at me when I'm talking to them. Isn't that the most disrespectful thing you could ever do to a person?"

The room was filled with mmm-hmmm's and nodding heads.

"Loud sighs and moans and groans," Bill added.

"Sucking teeth!" Miriam interjected.

"The raised eyebrow!" shouted Vicky.

There was such an overwhelming sense of unity in the room as everyone shared their personal non-verbal pet peeves that Haylie was almost sure that someone was going to stand up and shout "Hallelujah!" next, and everyone else would follow.

Attempting to regain control of her audience, Laura offered one of her own.

"Throwing your hand up in someone's face when they're talking to you!" she said.

"Oh yeah," Vicky chimed in. "I get that one from my kids! And don't forget the phrase that goes with it – 'talk to the hand 'cause I don't understand!' It doesn't get any more irritating than that!"

Donna rose out of her seat in her typical mother-bird-taking-charge stance, and turned around to face Vicky. "Honey, I got you an answer for that one. The next time your kids say that to you, you just turn around, put your hand on your rear end, and tell them 'talk to the booty 'cause the nurse is off duty!'"

And with that, the entire class was doubled over in laughter.

"Hallelujah!" Shouted Vicky from the back of the room.

Yep, I called it, thought Haylie to herself, but couldn't help but laugh along with the crowd anyway.

It took a few minutes for Laura to stop laughing and regain composure. By that time, several of the class participants were already practicing Donna's trick, and the sound of palms slapping rear ends echoed throughout the room, followed by laughter. At least they had accomplished a return demonstration, Laura was pleased to see.

At that point, she decided it was break time again.

***

Back in the classroom, the participants settled into their seats as Laura posed the next question. "How about a verbal affront? What is it, first of all, and how can you respond to it?"

"That's like making snide remarks or being really rude or abrupt," Brad offered. "And to respond to it… hmmm…. I honestly don't know."

The class was quiet for a moment. "I wouldn't know how to respond either if someone said something really rude and insulting to me," said Gena.

"Like being called one of the old and jealous nurses?" Miriam mumbled under her breath. Donna kicked her under the table.

Adriane volunteered a comment. "When someone says something ugly to you, there's usually more that they want to say. So how about just saying to them – 'please be direct with me.' Would that work?"

"It sounds good to me," Laura replied. "Moving along, let's talk about undermining activities. This reminds me of something that Donna mentioned earlier about her children... how they turn away and ignore her while she's trying to talk to them. They're deliberately ignoring her and undermining the importance of what she has to say to them. Does this ever happen among nurses?"

All heads nodded in unison.

"And how can we respond if it happens to us?"

The class collectively gave it some thought, and Mel was the first to respond. "How about, 'I was hoping you'd be able to listen to me and give me your attention right now. If this is a bad time for you, is there another time when we could talk and you could give me your full attention?"

Laura nodded. "Not bad, Mel. Or you could ask a question of the person who is undermining you. Something like, 'this isn't what I was expecting to happen and it leaves me with questions. Can you talk to me and help me understand?' Anyway, that's a fairly easy response compared to number nine on the list – sabotage."

Donna looked down at the floor again. "Like I did to Cathy," she said.

"Well, let's take that example," Laura said. "Let's say that Cathy found out that you never sent in the award nomination form. Put yourself in her shoes and tell me how she should deal with it."

"Well." Donna closed her eyes and massaged her temples, deep in thought. "If I were Cathy, I would have confronted me and asked why I did what I did."

"Okay," Laura said. "Can you think of a non-threatening way to do that?"

"Hmmm... not really. I mean, I'd be pretty upset."

"Of course you would be. Because you wouldn't understand why it was done. So perhaps you could say, 'there must be more to this situation than meets the eye. Can we talk in private about it?'"

Donna nodded. "And once I told her why I didn't submit the award nomination, do you think she would have understood? Do you think she would have forgiven me?" Donna's voice warbled, as if she was fighting the urge to cry.

"I can't say for sure," said Laura, "but if it had been me in that position, I really would have appreciated just getting your honest explanation. I think I would have felt relieved to know that it was never about me, but that it was about you."

"Exerting my power, to protect myself," Donna said. "Wrongfully so, but that's what was happening, right?"

"I think so," Laura replied, turning her attention back to the rest of the class. "But you recognize it now. And can prevent it from happening in the future. That's the important thing."

Donna nodded in agreement as Laura proceeded.

"We're down to our last in the list of the top ten. Withholding information."

Haylie looked up at Laura. "Like if your patient is diabetic, or is addicted to prescription pain medication, and no one tells you when you take over caring for the patient."

Nodding, Laura moved toward Haylie. "Great examples."

Miriam sighed loudly behind them.

"It's so important to communicate with each other and share information about your patients. Their outcomes depend on it. As nurses, you work as a team, and you're only as strong as the weakest link. Communication is what links you all together. If you keep that strong, your team will be strong, and your patients will benefit from it."

"So what should you do if someone withholds information?" Haylie asked.

"You confront them," Laura replied. "And tell them, 'I think that there was more information available. If I had known, it would have affected the way that I handled this situation.' What do you think?"

Haylie sat quietly for a moment. "It certainly makes the point," she said.

Behind her, Miriam was quiet.

"You all have done a great job today," Laura said, wrapping up the workshop. "Do any of you have questions? Or any comments? Anything you'd like to reflect upon from our discussion today?"

Haylie shifted in her seat as she finished jotting down notes. She thought for a moment, and then voiced the question on her mind. "Excuse me, Laura," she began, "I'm writing all of this down and it sounds easy enough to say in here while we're in the classroom, but once we get back into our work environment, is this really going to work? I mean… if I say these things to my co-workers, are they going to take me seriously or are they going to laugh at me? Or what if they think I'm being stuck up?"

Laura nodded to show that she understood Haylie's concerns. "You're asking great questions, Haylie, so I tell you what. Why don't we give this a try and see how it works in real life? Why don't you come up to the front of the room with me, Haylie? I've got an exercise that I think will help you."

Oh great, Haylie sighed as she stood up and made her way to the front of the room. *A dorky role play. That will teach me to keep my mouth shut next time.*

At the front of the room, Laura smiled at her mischievously. "So Haylie, did you hear that rumor going around about Gena?"

Gena giggled softly. "Make up a juicy one," she said from the back of the room. Laughter followed from the rest of the class.

"Um… no," Haylie said, grinning, and feeling awkward for having been involuntarily cast into the role of Anti-Lateral Violence Nurse Hero.

Laura leaned toward Haylie and dramatically held her hand up to her face, as if she were speaking in a hush, but whispered loudly enough for the rest of the class to hear. "Someone told me that she's been stealing narcotics, and she's going to get fired."

Laughing softly, Haylie played along. Imitating Laura, she lifted her own hand and cupped it around her mouth, and loudly whispered back, "Well, Gena's not around right now, and we shouldn't be talking about her like this behind her back."

Gasping, Laura took a step back. "Are you kidding me? What do you think this is, kindergarten? Come on, we're adults, Haylie. I'm only telling you because I know I can trust you and that you won't say anything back to her. Just thought you might like to know what Gena's really like when no one else is looking."

"Ooooh," someone in the audience murmured, acknowledging that Laura was putting Haylie on the spot with a challenging situation.

"Well," Haylie responded, pausing for a moment to think, "Here's the deal, Laura. If someone came to me and said something about YOU while you weren't around, especially something that could be really damaging to you, then I'd tell that person the same thing – that it's wrong to talk about people behind their backs. And I would HOPE that if someone said something about ME behind MY back to YOU, that you would do the same for me. So I think we both owe it to Gena to do the same. Rumors are rumors. What you heard about her may be true, or it may not. Regardless, it's none of my business and I don't want to talk about Gena like this when she's not around, so I think we should change the subject."

The room was filled with silence. Haylie looked at Laura, who stared back with a wide-eyed expression that she couldn't quite decipher. The rest of the class seemed to be holding their breath, waiting along with Haylie for the instructor's reaction.

"Haylie," she finally said, "You did an amazing job." She began to applaud, and the rest of the class did the same. Even Miriam, Haylie was surprised to see.

"You can have a seat now," Laura excused her. "But good for you. If you were getting graded on performance in this class, you would have just earned an A+ for critical thinking. You thought ahead and wondered how others would respond to the scripted responses. And, when put on the spot and you were challenged, you had to think hard about what to say, and you had to justify yourself. You really did a terrific job, Haylie."

"Yes she did," Donna echoed proudly.

Mel patted Haylie on the back, and Brad gave her a "thumbs up" sign.

Miriam looked smug, but was nodding anyway.

"Haylie," Laura continued, "Tell me how it felt to say those words to me."

"Easy, at first," Haylie responded. "When I responded to you the first time, I was just giving you the scripted response, and it felt… I don't know, safe, I guess, because we're here in the classroom, and you're the instructor who taught me to say it, so I knew I was doing exactly what I was supposed to. But when you got defensive and you didn't accept what I had to say, I really had to think about what I was going to say next."

"Right. And when you responded the second time, it came from your own thoughts and your own feelings, not from a script. You were saying it not just because it was what you were supposed to say. You were saying it because you really believed it was the right thing to say."

"Yeah," Haylie nodded with realization. "I guess so."

Laura smiled, then directed her attention to the rest of the class. "What you just saw may very well happen in real life once you start trying out these responses. Envision how others might respond to you, and be prepared to do some critical thinking. Changing a culture is tough work, and there may be some resistance when you go against the grain."

"So how do you know if it's worth it?" Brad asked. "Because I'll be honest, it's going to be really hard for me to try and say some of the things we've learned today. I'll be worried about the same things that Haylie just said a minute ago… will people laugh at me? Or think I'm being stuck up? Or what if they get defensive and accuse me of being a jerk? Why should I change everything unless I know it's going to make a difference?"

"Because it will make a difference," Laura said. "The responses that we're talking about right now are actually evidence-based. They were developed by a nurse named Martha Griffin, and put to the test on real nursing units in a hospital – just like your unit, Med-Surg South. After a while, the culture in those units changed. The violent behaviors stopped."

Brad nodded slowly. "Wow," he said thoughtfully. "I guess it is worth the effort, then."

Laura passed around a stack of wallet-size laminated cards with a hole punched in them, so that they could be kept behind name badges for quick reference.

"There's a blue card and a yellow card. Take one of each," she said. "Life is a stage, and there's no dress rehearsal. Which is why it's so important for you to know your lines. What we've spent the morning talking about today are actually scripted responses for cognitive rehearsal, and that's what you'll find on the blue card. These scripted phrases are designed to give you some standard responses for dealing with the lateral violence "Top Ten" as they come up. You don't have to repeat the phrases word for word, just so long as you get the general point across."

Haylie grabbed a blue and yellow card as the stack made its way to her. She looked at the blue card first. In super-small print, on both back and front, it read:

Prompting Card

Possible Pre-Rehearsed Response

1) Non verbal innuendo *(raising of the eyebrows, face making)*

- *I sense (I see from your facial expression) that there may be something you wanted to address with me, it is okay to speak with me directly.*

2) Verbal *(covert/overt)* ***affront*** *(snide remarks, lack of openness, abrupt responses)*

- *The individuals that I learn the most from are clearer in their directions and feedback. Is there some way we can structure this type of learning situation?*

- *That may be information that I don't need to know/hear, but what would help me is...*

3) Undermining activities *(turning away, not available)*

- *When an event happens that is contrary to that which was my understanding, it leaves me with questions. Help me to understand how this situation happened.*

4) Withholding information *(practice or patient)*

- *It is my understanding that there (is) was more information available regarding this situation, and I believe if I had known that, it would (will) affect how I handle what I learn or need to know*

5) Sabotage *(deliberate setting up of situation)*

- *There is more to this situation than meets the eye, could 'you and I' (whatever/whoever) meet in private and explore what happened?*

6) Infighting *(bickering with peers)* — *Open 'contentious' discussion is unprofessional and should be avoided*

- *This is not the time or place. Please stop (physically move to a neutral spot)*

- *I'm moving to another location*

7) **Scapegoating** *(attributing all that goes wrong to one individual) Rarely is one individual, one incident or one situation the cause for ALL that goes wrong, and scapegoating is an easy route to travel, but rarely solves problems*

  - *I don't think that this is the right connection*

8) **Backstabbing** *(complaining to others about an individual and not speaking with that individual). Like 'scapegoating' is maladaptive and nonproductive.*

  - *I don't feel right talking about "him/her/situation."*

9) **Failure to respect privacy**

  - *It bothers me to talk about that without their permission*
  - *I only overheard that and it shouldn't be repeated*

10) **Broken confidences**

  - *Wasn't that said in confidence?*
  - *That sounds like information that should remain confidential*
  - *He/she asked me to keep that confidential*

Griffin, M. (2004). Teaching cognitive rehearsal as a shield for lateral violence: An intervention for newly licensed nurses. *The Journal of Continuing Education in Nursing*, 35(6), 257-263. Used with permission.

Then Haylie read the yellow card:

Prompting Card

Universally Accepted Professional Working Behavior Rules

(To assist in making the best of work relationships)

  - *Accept one's fair share of the workload*
  - *Respect other's privacy*
  - *Be cooperative with regard to the shared physical working conditions (e.g. light, temperature, noise)*
  - *Be willing to help when requested*
  - *Keep confidences*
  - *Work cooperatively despite feelings of dislike*

- *Don't denigrate to superiors (speaking negatively about, have a pet name for, engage in negative conversations about)*
- *Address the co-workers by first name*
- *Ask for help and advise when necessary*
- *Look co-worker in the eye when having a conversation*
- *Don't be over-inquisitive about each other's private lives*
- *Repay debts, favors and compliments no matter how small*
- *Don't engage in conversation about a co-worker with another co-worker*
- *Stand up for the 'absent from conversation' co-worker when they are not present*
- *Don't criticize publicly*

Griffin, M. (2004). Teaching cognitive rehearsal as a shield for lateral violence: An intervention for newly licensed nurses. *The Journal of Continuing Education in Nursing,* 35(6), 257-263. Used with permission.

Wow, Haylie said to herself. *This is almost the exact opposite of what we do on Med-Surg South.*

"This is great information," Donna said. "Thank you, Laura."

"Yes, it is," Bill agreed, from the back of the room. "And I think that the most valuable lesson that I got out of this day is that we have to be responsible for ourselves as professionals. We can't go on 'eating our young' the way that animals do... the lions and tigers and-"

"Nurses, oh my!" Blurted out Gena.

Everyone laughed.

"Actually, I was going to say baboons," said Bill. "We're supposed to be the smarter, more evolved species, so we better start acting like it."

Heads nodded throughout the room.

"Any other comments or questions?" Laura offered one more time. "If not, then we're adjourned. Please make sure to fill out your evaluation form and drop it in the box in the back of the room, okay?"

She advanced to her last slide in her presentation. It was a simple quote on the screen:

> *"Be the change you wish to see in the world."*
> — *Mohandas Ghandi*

Laura's audience applauded, and went to work filling out their evaluations.

Haylie gave Laura a full sheet of "excellent" ratings. At the bottom of the page, she left a comment:

> *You don't know how much we need these scripts and the working behavior rules on my unit. Can you believe I just started this week, and I've already had thoughts of quitting? I promise, I am going to try the responses that you've taught us, and I'm going to do my best to follow the professional working behavior rules. I hope my other co-workers – and my preceptor – do too. Thanks, Laura!*

Chapter 11
The Following Monday

In her dream, Miriam was queen again.

Haylie knelt before her, looking smudged with dirt and disheveled. She was wearing an old potato sack and had her wrists bound with a piece of rope. She had just been escorted from the jail to stand before the queen and be judged for her crimes.

"Haylie Evans, you have been charged with posing as a nurse, while you are nothing more than a court jester. Your professionalism is laughable… and your level of competency is a joke! Have you anything to say for yourself?" Miriam barked out.

Haylie wept. "I'm a good nurse, Miriam, I am. I'm trying as hard as I can."

Miriam grunted. "Trying is not good enough." She stood up from her throne and raised her royal scepter toward the sky. "Off with her head!"

She expected the kingdom to reply with a jubilant shout, and much applause, but instead, an odd thing began to happen. The crowd began to part, leaving a path of clear ground in the middle, leading all the way up to Miriam's throne.

Through the cleared path came the two white, royal horses, followed by the chariot. And standing upon it was Homer, guiding the horses, reins in his hands.

"Homey?" Miriam asked.

Haylie shuffled aside as the two horses led him to Miriam's throne, where he paused and bowed to her. "Good day, my queen," he said to her, flashing a radiant smile.

"Homey!" Miriam stood up from her throne, tossing her scepter aside. "You can talk normally again! And you can smile! What happened?"

He turned and looked over his shoulder, up toward the sky. "It's time for me to go, my dear. There's somewhere else I have to be. It has been a wonderful journey with you, Miriam, and you'll always be queen in my heart. Good bye for now, my dear."

He snapped the reins and the horses spun around, leading him away from Miriam and down the cleared path. Then the horses sprouted wings and began to fly, picking up Homer's chariot with a sharp jolt that caught him off guard. He stumbled and staggered as the chariot went airborne, and loudly yelled out his favorite curse word – this time without the lisp. When he regained his footing, he raised his hand into the sky and waved at Miriam as he soared away.

Miriam opened her eyes. Looking at the clock on her nightstand, she saw that it was just a few minutes before four o'clock in the morning. An unsettled feeling came over her.

"Homey?" She reached over and touched her husband's shoulder. He didn't respond.

"Homey?" She shook him gently. Once, then again. And then, more forcefully. She touched his face, and it was cold.

"Oh Homer…"

***

Haylie had awakened at four o'clock in the morning and couldn't get back to sleep, somehow feeling in her gut that something wasn't quite right.

She stared at the ceiling, wondering what kind of excuse she could come up with to call in today.

Hi Donna, it's Haylie. I'm sick today. Stomach flu.

No. Too gross.

Hi Donna, it's Haylie. I can't come in today. My car broke down and don't know what's wrong with it, and I don't know how long it will take me to get it fixed.

No good either. Knowing Donna and how motherly she was, she'd probably offer to come pick Haylie up and give her a ride to work.

Hi Donna, it's Haylie. I can't come in today because Miriam is making my life a living hell, and I honestly don't think I can spend another twelve hours around her without causing serious bodily harm to her, and any innocent bystanders. Could you please talk her into retiring already? Or maybe move her to another shift? Another unit? I would be so happy, and I could do such a good job if she wasn't there…

If only she could be that honest.

Maybe I should just quit.

As she had written on her evaluation at the lateral violence class, it certainly wasn't the first time that the thought had crossed her mind, and she promised to revisit it and give it more consideration once she got through with her twelve hour shift.

Stepping off of the elevator, Haylie walked onto the floor of Med-Surg South. Her work day was beginning whether she liked it or not.

At the nurse's station, Mel and Donna stood closely together, talking in concerned, hushed voices. A couple of other nurses from other units were also there. Brad was on the phone, talking in a low voice and looking very serious. Haylie immediately knew something was wrong.

"Donna? What's going on?" She asked, as she approached the cluster of worried nurses.

Donna reached out and took Haylie's hand, pulling her into the circle. "Miriam's husband died early this morning. She's going to be out for a while. We're talking about coverage right now."

Haylie's stomach felt sick.

Poor Miriam, she thought to herself. Guilt suddenly washed over her. Just a few short hours ago, she had been wishing that Miriam could just disappear from Med-Surg South and be out of her way. But she would have never wished this on Miriam. She sank down into a chair and stared down at the floor.

"Haylie… are you okay?" Donna asked.

"You're looking a little pale," Mel commented. "Are you upset by the news?"

She nodded. "I guess. I'm worried about Miriam. Is she okay?"

"She's alright," Donna assured her. "She was expecting it. She knew Homer wasn't going to get any better. They both did. All of his arrangements were made, so at least that's taken care of and she doesn't have to worry about it."

Haylie blinked several times. Her vision was becoming blurry. She reached up and was surprised to find tears in her eyes.

What? She wondered. *Why am I crying? I never even met Homer... and I pretty much hate Miriam...*

Mel handed her a tissue, and Donna knelt down to hug her.

"Surprising, isn't it? That you actually feel something for Miriam?" Donna asked Haylie.

"Well... yeah," she responded, blotting her eyes.

"It's not such a horrible thing to find out that you care," said Donna.

"Yeah, but for Miriam? Who would've thought?" Haylie said, laughing softly. "It just doesn't seem natural."

"You're a nurse," Donna said. "You care about everyone. Especially those who are hurting. It's the most natural thing in the world for you."

Behind the nurse's desk, Brad finished a phone conversation and hung up. "That was Miriam's son. Visitation is at the funeral home tomorrow night beginning at seven o'clock. The funeral will be the day after at ten in the morning."

"I'll be there at both," Haylie said. "And Donna, whatever else I can do, please let me know. I just want to help."

Chapter 12
Wednesday

They went to the visitation and the funeral together, all four of them. And although none of them knew Homer all that well, Donna, Mel and Brad all blotted their eyes during his graveside service. Haylie felt the urge to cry a couple of times during the eulogy, but fought it. She felt that since she had never met Homer, she would be crying just for the sake of crying, just because everyone else was, and she didn't want to do that.

However, when Miriam rose from her seat and went to Homer's casket, where she rested her head upon the wooden box and whispered something to her husband that no one else could hear, Haylie could hold back no longer. She went through her entire wad of tissues from her purse first, then she exhausted Mel's supply, and then Donna's. Finally, Brad took off his suit jacket and handed it to her. He put his arm around her and hugged her to his side while she snuffled and wept into his jacket's collar.

***

Mel decided to stick around the cemetery after everyone else had left. Even Miriam. She sat in front of Homer's casket, staring out at the sea of headstones all around her in Dogwood Memorial Cemetery.

Life is so short... she thought to herself.

She looked up toward the sun. It was a bright and beautiful day.

Not fair, Mel thought. *Beautiful sunshine on a day of mourning and loss.*

It's like you're mocking us down here, God. What's up with that?
A strong wind came from nowhere, ruffling Mel's long, dark hair that she normally wore pulled up in a ponytail.

So you're still there, I see. Just letting me know that you're still around, are you?

The wind died away as quickly as it had come. A cloud passed over the sunshine, and the cemetery turned gray for a moment.

We haven't talked in a while, have we? I've been so mad at you, you know. You gave me this wonderful, perfect dream life, and then you took it away from me. Why?

She waited for another gust of wind, but it didn't come.

Now Amanda has the life I used to have. She got my husband, my house, my car... and my kids even like her. Why, God? I didn't do anything wrong, did I? I was faithful. I was always a good wife and a good mother, and I've been a good nurse and I've helped so many people...

So what in the world did I do to deserve this pain?

A gust of wind breezed by her again, and the cloud that had covered the sun quickly passed. Once again, the cemetery was filled with warmth and light.

So what are you trying to tell me? The sun will come out tomorrow? Who are you up there anyway... God, or little orphan Annie?

Another strong breeze blasted her face, sending her hair flying in every direction once again.

I don't understand! I need a sign. Did I do something wrong that I don't realize? Have you turned your back on me? Are you punishing me?

She waited. Where was all of this wind coming from all of a sudden? It had been mildly breezy during the ceremony, but nothing compared to now.

Or have you given me this pain for a reason? Are you trying to teach me something? Is this helping me grow into a stronger and better person somehow? Am I where I'm supposed to be at this point in my life? Am I? Send me a sign. Please, a sign!

This time, the gust of wind was so strong that it nearly knocked her over. She struggled to stand up, and clawed at her face to clear the hair from her eyes. And suddenly, she felt herself being pelted all over by some kind of small objects...

Uh oh, is this my sign? What are you throwing at me? Garbage? Rotten tomatoes?

Wrestling her hair behind her head, she quickly wrapped it into a bun at the nape of her neck and knotted it in place. With her view unobstructed, she looked down the length of her body to the small objects that had assaulted her in the wind.

Dogwood blossoms.

They were everywhere.

The wind had lifted them from the trees that were planted throughout the cemetery, and they were scattered all over the ground, forming a jagged ring around Mel's feet.

"Oh..." she gasped, as a blossom fluttered into her hand.

And she waited for a long moment.

Thank you, she prayed.

For the first time in years, Imelda Tagaro felt the presence of something unusual in her heart.

Something she had forgotten how to embrace and feel and hope for; something she had given up on a long time ago.

It was peace.

Chapter 13
The Next Monday

Donna felt like a week was too soon for Miriam to return to work. Not only was she concerned that Miriam wasn't ready to resume work again; she had enjoyed how calm things had been on the unit the prior week, while the war between Miriam and Haylie was at a cease fire.

But Miriam had returned, ready to jump back into work, and no one could talk her out of it.

She wasn't her normal gruff self, everyone noticed. Her voice was monotone, and her facial expressions were flat. She seemed hollow and numb.

"I'm worried about Miriam," Mel said, leaning over the desk at the nurse's station, just after Miriam stepped away to give meds to one of her patients.

"We all are," echoed Brad. "She's like a ghost. Like she's here but she's not really here, if you know what I mean? It's Miriam's body, without Miriam's personality inside."

"She's probably still in shock," said Donna.

Haylie stood behind them, listening. She felt that her best strategy for now – given Miriam's aversion to her – was just to avoid Miriam, and any conversations or thoughts about her altogether.

"Yeah, well, it's kind of nice to have her acting kind of comatose instead of her normal grouchy self," Mel said, laughing a bit.

"Yeah, you said it," Brad agreed. "The quiet Miriam is kind of scary. Wonder if she's headed for a nervous breakdown or something?"

And then Haylie did something that surprised even herself. "Hey... guys, isn't that kind of mean?"

Brad and Mel exchanged a confused glance.

"I guess what I mean..." Haylie struggled for the right words, "is that Miriam's not here, and we're talking about her. And... we shouldn't."

Haylie took a deep breath. *Did I really just say that? Did I really just defend Miriam and try to protect her privacy?*

Mel and Brad looked up at her, and then at each other.

"Haylie is right," Donna said, a smile slowly crossing her face. "She's absolutely, one hundred percent right. Good for you," she complimented Haylie.

And then Mel nodded. "You are right, Haylie."

Even Brad agreed with a quick nod. "Yeah," he said. "It's so easy to fall back on old habits," he said. "But it's no excuse." He dragged his thumb and index finger across his lips as if he were zipping them shut.

Donna patted Haylie on the back. "I'm proud of you for stepping up and saying that," she said. "Nice job. See the power of one? All it took was you to say and do the right thing, and you set us all straight."

Grinning, Haylie felt as if an incredible weight had suddenly been lifted off of her shoulders.

***

Haylie sat at the nurse's station, making notes in a patient's chart.

Miriam rounded the corner and dropped a new chart in front of her. She flipped it open and pointed to a page with Haylie's handwriting on it. "I was reviewing your notes," she said. "There's an abbreviation in here that's inappropriate."

"Okay," Haylie said, avoiding the urge to get defensive. "Which one?"

"Right here," Miriam said, pointing in the chart, "It says right here, 'patient out of bed with 'ass.' Well, I would hope so, Haylie. That would be a horrible thing to leave behind in the bed, wouldn't it?" Her tone was sharp, and her words were dripping with sarcasm.

Haylie sighed.   "It stands for 'assistance.'   I think you realize that."

"It's not an approved abbreviation." She marked through Haylie's writing with her pen and wrote the correct abbreviation for assistance.

"Well thank you," Haylie said. "Thank you for slashing through my 'ass' and showing me the error of my ways." She hadn't intended to be sarcastic in return – it just happened.

Miriam snarled. "If only you were half as cute and funny as you think you are, Haylie… there might be a more promising career for you as a comedian."

"If only," she said, in mock agreement.

Miriam closed the chart and sank down onto the seat next to Haylie. She sighed deeply, and then closed her eyes.

Uh oh, thought Haylie. *How dramatic. There must be a big show coming up next! Tune in to the Miriam Simpson show on the Lateral Violence channel, folks…*

And then Miriam leaned forward, bracing her elbows on the counter, and sinking her face into her hands. She huffed and puffed loudly.

"Miriam?" Haylie asked, suddenly growing alarmed.

Miriam tilted her head up, and Haylie saw that her face was beet red.

"Oh my God! What's wrong? Miriam? Are you okay?" Haylie shot up out of her seat. "Donna… Mel!" She cried out, longing for someone else to come and take charge.

Brad rounded the corner. "They just went down to lunch. It's just us up here."

Haylie began speaking quickly and urgently. "Miriam's having some kind of episode. She and I were sitting here talking and then she just sank down into the chair, put her head in her hands for a second, and when she looked up, her face got all red like this…" she pointed to Miriam.

"She needs to go downstairs to the E.D. I'm calling down there right now."

Haylie sat down and faced Miriam. She pulled one of her hands away from her face and placed her index and middle finger just on the inside of Miriam's wrist to check her pulse.

"Miriam, can you talk to me?" Haylie asked?

Breathing heavily through pursed lips, Miriam nodded and weakly said "yeah."

"Okay," Haylie began. "Your pulse is way too fast and is very thready. Do you know what's going on? Has this happened before?"

Miriam nodded. "Blood pressure, I think. It happens sometimes. Usually not this strong."

"Alright," Haylie said. "Are you having chest pain? Or pain anywhere else?"

Miriam shook her head from side to side.

"Feeling dizzy?"

Miriam nodded. "Yes. Tingly in my fingers and hands and toes."

"You're hyperventilating," Haylie said. "You've got to slow down your breathing. Can you breathe slower? Try it. Deep, slow breaths."

Miriam closed her eyes and shook her head from side to side.

"Come on Miriam, you know how to do this. You were the one that showed me how. In through the nose, out through the mouth. Come on. Do it with me. In through the nose, out through the mouth…"

She followed Haylie's instructions and her breathing slowed a little bit.

"Keep doing that Miriam. Good job. Now tell me what meds you're on."

"Beta…" Miriam huffed and puffed, "Beta blocker… Lasix…"

Haylie started making notes on a scratch pad in front of her. "Okay," she said. "Did you take them today?"

Miriam closed her eyes for a moment and then opened them again. "Don't remember," she said. "Don't remember."

"Keep breathing – in through the nose, out through the mouth. Gotta slow it down."

Brad looked up from the phone. "I'm on the phone with Emergency," he continued, in a frustrated tone. "I told them we've got one of our own up here that needs to be seen, but they don't have a single bed open right now. There was a huge multi-car crash earlier today, and they've got people with fractures, lacerations, all kinds of bad stuff, sitting all over the place down there, waiting to be seen. They don't even have so much as a wheelchair open."

"Well we've got bed 3-A open right now, we can lay her down there, just for now," said Haylie, "but we need someone from down there to come up and check her out."

Brad shook his head. "They said they can't spare anyone right now. Not unless we're calling a code."

"Then get off the phone. I need your help. Go get a wheelchair so we can get her into bed 3-A."

Brad hung up the phone and did as Haylie directed.

Together they helped load Miriam into the wheelchair and pushed her to the empty bed.

"Miriam, what do we need to do for you?" Haylie asked.

Miriam shrugged. "Can't think... head spinning."

"Lie back then and try to relax until we can get you to the E.D.," Haylie ordered. She raised up the head of the bed slightly and guided Miriam back onto the pillow. Brad grabbed a cuff and fastened it around Miriam's arm, then pressed the button on the console to begin inflating it.

Haylie looked at her, feeling helpless. *Think*, she commanded herself. *What now?*

Miriam's mouth opened, and she tried to speak. Her lips smacked, but no sound came out. Her mouth had to have been all dried out from all of the huffing and puffing, Haylie figured.

Dried out.

"When was the last time you had something to eat or drink?" Haylie asked.

Miriam shrugged. "Yesterday, I think," she mouthed. "I haven't been eating or drinking that much since Homer died."

The blood pressure cuff deflated and the monitor beeped,

displaying her numbers. They were quite low.

"That's a big part of the problem. You're dehydrated," Haylie determined. "And probably starving, too. I'm going to get you something to eat and drink."

She raced out of the room and returned with a pitcher of water and a cinnamon roll.

Miriam didn't have to be coached. She took several sips of water, and Haylie refilled her cup. She ate a few bites of the cinnamon roll and then put it down, chasing it with another full glass of water. Then she rested her head back on the pillow, sipped another glass of water down, and closed her eyes.

Her breathing wasn't so labored, finally, and had almost returned to normal.

"You feel better now?" Brad asked.

"Yeah," she replied.

"Good. I was getting ready to stick you and start an IV," he joked.

"In your dreams," Miriam said.

They sat quietly for a moment, waiting with Miriam while she rested and drank more water.

Haylie checked her pulse again, and found that it had grown slower and stronger. The color of her face was returning to normal.

Just then, a CNA in the signature red scrubs from the Emergency Room appeared in the doorway of the room. "Heard you got a nurse having some problems up here. I'm assuming it's you?" She asked Miriam.

Nodding, Miriam pulled the cuff off and steadied herself on her feet. "Yeah, I'm feeling better now, but I'm still going to get seen anyway."

"It may be a while before we get around to seeing you, but I'll take you down there if you'd like to come with me."

"Fine with me," Miriam agreed.

Miriam accompanied the CNA back to Emergency in a wheelchair.

Brad and Haylie returned to the nurse's desk, relieved.

"You did a great job," Brad said. "I was actually pretty impressed."

Haylie smiled. "Thanks. I thought I did okay too. But Miriam was right there in the middle of it, and she had nothing positive to say to me. Not even 'thanks for trying to help me, Haylie.' I didn't even get that much."

"Yeah, I know," Brad said, "She's just really hard on the new folks, that's all. I remember when I first started here a few years ago. It seems like a long time ago, but it really wasn't. I remember what it was like to be a new nurse. You'll get the hang of it."

Shrugging, Haylie sank into a chair and went back to charting. "I'm not so sure about that, Brad. It was different for you. You did take care of patients in the military, and I know it was different in a lot of ways, but you at least came in with some experience. You were never really all that 'new'... you know?"

"Oh, but I was. I had Miriam as a preceptor, too, and I was new enough as far as she was concerned. And she was hard on me. Trust me, I was in your shoes and I know just what it's like. She spends more time telling you what you've done wrong than what you've done right, but in reality, she sees everything that you do, Haylie. She pays attention. She knows you're a good nurse."

"I doubt she thinks so. And even if she did, she'd never tell me, not in a million years. She hates me."

"No she doesn't," Brad insisted. "And she does know that you're a good nurse. One of these days she'll tell you how she really feels, and what she really thinks. I promise. That day will come."

Haylie frowned and shook her head from side to side. "I don't know if I can survive here that long."

"Oh come on. Cheer up," Brad said with a smile. "You're not alone. I guess this is something that we all have to go through when we're new nurses. No one seems to escape it. Everyone has stories about this kind of stuff. Everyone has their own Miriam when they're starting out."

Haylie shook her head. "But why? It shouldn't have to be that way," she said. "Isn't that the whole point of the class that we took?"

***

In the early evening, it was eerily quiet on the unit. Most of the patients were sleeping. Except for Mr. Eldridge, who was watching another episode of "Pimp My Ride." Brad wandered into his room to check on him.

"Brad!" He said with excitement. "My favorite nurse! So good to see you. At long last, you get to meet my lovely wife, Regina." Mr. Eldridge motioned to his wife seated at his bedside. Regina was pretty, just as he had promised, with sparkling blue eyes and shoulder-length graying hair.

"Hello," she said to Brad, "Thank you for taking such good care of my husband. He's a pain the neck, isn't he?" She squeezed her husband's hand.

Brad laughed. "Not at all. I really like him. I don't mind taking care of him at all."

"I'll remember that the next time I get tired of taking care of him," Regina laughed. "I'll just bring him right back! And you can spoon feed him jello and stay up all night long with him while he watches MTV at a volume loud enough for people in Timbuktu to hear!"

Mr. Eldridge tugged on her hand, pulling her toward him. He kissed her on the cheek. "I'm not all that bad, am I?" Then he turned to Brad as his wife kissed him back. "My old lady… she adores me. She'll just never let on."

"Oh, he's full of poop," she said. "That's why you good folks had to go put an ostomy on him, isn't it? He's so full of it, he's gotta squeeze it out of his side now into a little baggie."

"Hey, love me, love my poop," said Mr. Eldridge.

Brad laughed again and waved at the elderly couple as he left the room. "Nice to meet you, Regina."

"Likewise, honey!" She called out to him.

Brad felt a sinking sensation in his stomach, and he couldn't figure out why. Back at the nurse's station, he paused to sit down for a minute and rest his head in his hands.

Only one thought crossed his mind.

Sue.

In thirty or so years, when it came time for him to be lying in a hospital bed, who would be there at his side?

Probably not Mel. She would be remarried by that point, with a new life of her own, and not as much time to devote to her friends.

Probably not his best friend Sam. He'd be spending his days playing video games and guzzling beer well into his old age.

And hopefully not Biff the Rottweiler.

Sue.

He missed her so much. Maybe he'd been wrong about everything. Maybe he *was* ready to settle down with her, start a family, think about his future…

He went to the phone and dialed Sue's number. He was relieved when she answered. The sound of her voice was music to his ears.

"I miss you," was all that he said.

She hesitated for a moment, and then replied. "I miss you too."

Relief washed over him. "Can I see you? Tonight, maybe? After work?"

"Okay," she said.

"Dinner at La Fiesta? Eight o'clock?"

"Sure," she accepted. "And Brad, this time I promise… I won't—"

"Empty a pitcher of margaritas over my head?" Brad smiled.

Embarrassed, Sue chuckled softly. "I was going to say 'leave you.' I won't walk out on you this time. But as far as the margaritas, no promises there."

He laughed softly. "I'm looking forward to seeing you."

"Me too."

Chapter 14
Tuesday

As she parked her car and made her way up to Med-Surg South, Haylie's cell phone beeped. She flipped it open to find that there was a new message from Isabel.

Did U find a date 2 my wedding yet? Mom wants 2 know!!!

Here we go again, Haylie thought to herself. Stepping into the elevator, she threw her phone into her purse and sighed.

"Wait, hold the door!" She heard a male voice cry from down the hallway. Haylie hit the "door open" button and the doors retracted. A young man in red scrubs, whom she immediately recognized, stepped into the elevator with her.

"Hi Dan!" She said. "How are things going for you since graduation?"

He grinned at her. "Hey, Haylie. It's good to see you! Things are going okay, I guess. I'm just trying to get used to life in the fast lane down in the E.D. There's never a dull moment, that's for sure! How are things going for you on Med-Surg South?"

Trying not to appear too distressed, Haylie forged a smile. "Oh, they're... just fine, I guess."

Dan smiled. "It's hard, being the new kid on the block, trying to fit in and make friends. I know, you're probably going through the same things that I am."

"Yeah. Some of the older nurses here…" She almost launched into a conversation about Miriam, but the elevator doors closed, reminding her that she needed to push a button – and shut her mouth before she started talking about her colleague behind her back. "Ooops, sorry," Haylie said. "What floor?"

"Third," Dan replied.

"Cool. Me too." She pressed the button for the third floor. Then she looked at Dan again.

He's really cute, she suddenly found herself thinking. But he's gay!

And then a fantastic thought dawned upon her. *Maybe he'd be my date to Isabel's wedding? No one would ever know that he's gay and that he already has a love interest of his own. I wouldn't have to tell anyone! They could think that he was my, Mister Right, and just leave me alone for a change.*

"Hey Dan," she blurted out, "Any chance you might want to be my date at my sister's wedding this Saturday?"

His eyes lit up. "Yeah. Actually I'd be honored. Thanks for asking."

Haylie was so excited she clapped her hands. "Awesome," she said with relief. "Thanks soooo much. My mom has been giving me such grief about finding a date. You've totally saved me!"

"No problem," he replied. "It would be cool to hang out with you again! We've hardly talked at all since we finished nursing school."

"Yeah, we'll have fun," Haylie nodded. "And tell Eric thanks for letting me borrow you for a day!"

Dan suddenly looked confused. His brow wrinkled, and he frowned as if he didn't understand.

Oops, thought Haylie. *Apparently I just said the wrong thing.*

"Why would Eric mind if you borrow me for a day?" He asked. And then a look of realization crossed his face. "Oh… hey, you don't think that Eric and I are-"

"Oh no, of course not," Haylie replied, a little too quickly. "Well, actually… yeah, I did."

Dan laughed. "It's okay. You're not the first person to think we're gay. We're just good friends and roommates, nothing more. We have separate bedrooms and we share the rent equally…. Promise," he said with a smile.

Open mouth, insert foot, Haylie scolded herself. "Dan, I'm so sorry. I feel like an idiot."

"It's okay," he said. "It's human nature, Haylie. What we don't know about each other, we fill in the blanks with whatever makes the most sense to us."

"Well, it stinks. I really need to stop making assumptions about people. It's just plain stupid."

Dan grinned. "It's okay. I forgive you. And guess what? You can make it up to me. Eric's getting married in a few months himself and I'm going to need a date to his wedding. So I'm hoping you'll return the favor."

"I'd be glad to," Haylie replied.

"So it's a date," Dan said, as the elevator doors opened. "Can I call you sometime before then?"

Haylie thought for a minute, and then nodded. "Yeah," she said. "Sure. I'll email you my phone number, okay?"

"Awesome!"

They stepped off the elevator together and went their separate ways.

So... Dan Matcher wasn't gay after all.

Hadn't Miriam told her as much?

"I really am an idiot," Haylie said to herself.

***

When Haylie arrived on the nursing unit, she went to the break room. Miriam was there, eating a donut and sipping coffee.

"Hi," said Haylie, not knowing what else to say.

"Hello," Miriam responded.

"Are you feeling better?"

Miriam looked up and nodded. "Yes, I am, thanks."

Haylie waited for her to continue, but she didn't. "So I'm

just curious," she prompted Miriam, "what exactly happened to you yesterday?"

"An anxiety attack, the doctor thinks," she said. "By the time they saw me in Emergency, my blood pressure was normal, my EKG results were normal, labs were normal, and I felt fine all over. I'm supposed to follow up with my doctor in a few days and see if he thinks I should get more tests done, but the latest word is that I'm fine. Just need to learn how to manage my stress better."

Haylie wondered if Miriam was suggesting that she was somehow to blame, but refrained from posing the question. "I'm glad you're better today," she said.

"Thank you," Miriam replied.

Oddly enough, it felt like a civil conversation. But Haylie had been fooled before by Miriam acting politely toward her. She didn't want to get burned again, and felt that the best thing she could do would be to stay out of Miriam's path. "I need to go see what patients I have today," she said, and left the room.

***

Haylie went to her patient in bed 3-B and woke him from a sound sleep. "Good morning, Mr. Cole. My name is Haylie. I'm going to be your nurse today. I'm sorry to wake you, but I read over your chart this morning and saw that the doctor ordered some medicine for you. I need to start an IV on you, okay?"

Mr. Cole nodded and closed his eyes again, as Haylie went to work starting the IV.

Had Miriam's ears deceived her?

She had tiptoed down the hall behind Haylie and now stood there listening outside of room 3.

"Good morning, Mr. Cole. My name is Haylie..." Miriam overheard. "... I read over your chart this morning..."

Haylie actually read her patient's chart? Miriam thought.

And she was getting ready to start an IV. This Miriam had to see.

She craned her neck and poked her head slightly into the room.

Bed A was empty, and the curtain separating the two was open, so Miriam had a clear view of Haylie and the patient in Bed B.

She watched as Haylie carefully donned a pair of latex gloves, gathered the supplies to start an IV, prepped the site, and stuck the patient.

Good, Miriam almost said aloud. She couldn't deny it. Haylie was doing a good job.

And just when she expected Haylie to gather up the trash and peel off her gloves, she received the surprise of her life.

Haylie tore a small strip of tape from the roll she kept on her stethoscope, and then tore a small notch at each end. She pressed the piece of tape down over the line, fitting the tubing between the notches. "It helps hold it in place," she explained to her patient. "This makes it a little more comfortable for you, and it will make it easier for me to remove it when it's time for your line to come out." And then Haylie exhaled deeply, as if she had been holding her breath the entire time.

"Let me show you a little trick," Miriam suddenly recalled herself saying to Haylie, just a couple of weeks ago. Miriam felt her face blush, and a strange sensation rising in her chest.

Miriam wondered... *was it pride?* That she had shaped the future of this young woman, by passing on a small trick of the trade that would become part of her legacy as a nurse?

If not pride, then what else? Was it sadness, maybe? Was it a bittersweet reminder that she was on her way out, and was having to share her best secrets with her replacement?

Or was it maybe a little bit of both?

Chapter 15
Wednesday

In the elevator, Haylie paused before pushing the button to the third floor, hopeful that Dan would round the corner and she'd see him again, if only for a few minutes. She pressed the "door open" button instead.

It had been a long, long time since she had dated anyone. She hadn't realized until just yesterday how focused on nursing she had been. For the past few years, her life had been consumed with nursing school. After school, she had studied around the clock until she took her boards and passed them. Then, she had dedicated herself to finding a job. And since she had been hired by Dogwood, she'd thought of little else outside of her role as the new nurse on Med-Surg South. No time for dating or boyfriends during her long journey into the field of nursing.

But now... she was ready. Since she had talked to Dan yesterday morning, she hadn't been able to stop thinking about his sparkling eyes and his wavy brown hair. And the way that he smiled when she asked him to be her date to her sister's wedding.

BEEEEEEEEEEEP! The elevator fussed loudly at her, letting her know that she'd been holding the doors open for much too long.

"Hold it, please!" Cried a voice from around the corner. Not Dan's unfortunately. It was a female voice, muffled by the sound of shuffling feet. Two other young nurses rounded the corner and joined her in the elevator. Haylie thought that she recognized one of them, a tall girl with short red hair, from one of her orientation classes. "Thanks," they said. "Fourth floor."

Haylie pressed buttons three and four and leaned against the wall of the elevator as they started their journey up into the hospital.

"So as I was saying," the red-haired nurse said to the other, "That Brad guy... adorable. I would totally go out with him, if he were available."

Haylie grinned. *Guess I'm not the only one with guys on the brain,* she thought to herself. *Wonder if it's our Brad from Med-Surg South?*

"Tell me about it," the other nurse responded to her friend. "He is sooooo hot. I hope that girl Mel knows how lucky she is.""

Whoa, thought Haylie. *They ARE talking about our Brad. AND our Mel, too.*

"Oh, I don't know about that," said the redhead. "I hear she's twice his age or something. I bet he's just fooling around with her and she takes the whole thing more seriously than he does."

"Yeah, I doubt she's his one and only. I hear he's got some other girlfriend that works at Hallmark. Probably a real airhead. I bet she has no clue that he's messing around with one of his co-workers."

They giggled, as the elevator doors opened. They stepped aside to let Haylie pass, and she walked between them. Stepping out of the elevator, she felt her face redden with anger. *How dare they talk about my friends that way?*

The elevator doors began to close as the redhead nurse and her friend continued to laugh away, at Brad and Mel's expense.

No, Haylie said to herself. *This is wrong.*

She whirled around and shoved her hand between the elevator doors, just before they snapped shut. The doors tapped her hand lightly on both sides, and quickly retracted open again. The two nurses stopped laughing and stared at Haylie, confused.

"Excuse me," she said. "I don't mean to butt into your conversation, but Brad and Mel are my co-workers... and my friends. They're entitled to their privacy and their personal lives just like the rest of us. And regardless of what you think you know about them, it's not fair for you to spread rumors and talk about them that way."

The redhead's jaw dropped, and she blinked several times. Her friend's face turned a deep shade of red.

"We're sorry," the redhead finally said. She looked embarrassed. "No offense, okay?"

Haylie nodded. "Yeah. No offense." She smiled to show that she meant it. "Thanks," she said, as she removed her hand. The elevator doors closed again. From behind them, Haylie heard one of the nurses mumble, "Well, that was embarrassing."

Haylie smiled slightly as she thought about what Laura said in the lateral violence class.

"After enough people start voicing their discontent with the top ten lateral violence behaviors, and they keep doing it for long enough, then it's no longer easy, safe – or even practical for that matter – for people to continue those behaviors."

***

Donna closed the door to her office and relaxed into her chair for a moment of calm before her workday started. A letter had arrived yesterday, and it made her pray with thanksgiving and smile and cry and hug Sean, all at the same time. A space had opened up on the wait list, and he had been accepted to the University of North Carolina at Chapel Hill.

She hadn't heard from Darius yet. She had sent the money a couple of weeks ago and was fairly confident that he had received it already. She prayed that he would call her, but he didn't. She didn't expect a letter back from him. Not until he needed money again, anyway. And since she hadn't obliged his last request for $200, she wondered if she'd hear back from him at all.

Donna picked up a small framed picture of her three children from her desk. It was at least ten years old. Jeannie had just been a toddler. She was sitting on Sean's lap, and Darius was standing behind them, with one hand on each of their shoulders. She picked up the picture and held it over her heart, squeezing it tightly.

Dear Lord, please bless my babies. You know what I pray for, day in and day out, dear Lord, and I know that not all of my prayers will be answered. Not the way that I want them to be answered, anyway. But I do ask you to keep them safe and well. Help them, dear Lord, to adjust to changes in life, and to overcome their limitations. And may they always be there for each other, dear Lord. Life is too lonely to go it alone. Let us be a family, dear Lord. Please bless my children.

She put the picture down on her desk and clasped her hands together, and prayed again.

This time, for the nurses on her unit.

Dear Lord, please bless my nurses. You know what I pray for, day in and day out, dear Lord, and I know that not all of my prayers will be answered. Not the way that I want them to be answered, anyway.

She thought for a moment about Miriam, and worried for her health.

But I do ask you to keep them safe and well.

She thought about Haylie. So new, so hopeful, so full of spirit, but still so lacking in skill and judgment.

Help them, dear Lord, to adjust to changes in life, and to overcome their limitations.

She thought of Brad and Mel, for the big-sister and little-brother kind of friendship that they shared. How they always seemed to be able to understand and lean on one another.

And may they always be there for each other, dear Lord.

Then she thought about Miriam again, having recently lost her beloved husband. She thought about Mel, struggling with the pain of her recent divorce. She thought about Brad, and his on-again off-again relationship with his girlfriend. She thought about Haylie, who had come to Med-Surg South looking for friendship, but instead had been the brunt of lateral violence.

And then she thought about herself. Like Miriam, a widow. And a mother whose babies were growing up way too quickly, spreading their wings and flying away, some in directions that she would not have chosen for them. In just a few years, little Jeannie would be grown and gone from the house too. And then she would be alone.

*Life is too lonely to go it alone. Let us be a family, dear Lord.
Please bless my nurses. Amen.*

Chapter 16
Thursday

Haylie arrived at Med-Surg South with a smile on her face. Dan had called her last night, and they had talked for nearly two hours. He was nice. Really nice. And someone that Haylie could actually see herself dating someday – maybe. For now, though, it was nice just to have a friend.

She went into the break room, where Brad was sitting at the computer browsing the Internet.

"Can I check my email when you're done?" Haylie asked.

"Sure, I'll only be here just another minute or two."

"No problem," Haylie said. She couldn't help but notice that Brad was looking at diamond solitaire rings. "Whoa," she said, "are those engagement rings you're looking at?"

Brad turned around and grinned. "Yeah," he said. "Sue and I are working our way toward getting back together."

Haylie smiled. "So you guys are going to get engaged?"

"Well… not right now," he said, "but eventually, maybe. I'm just trying to figure out how much a decent ring is going to cost me, so I'll know how long I've got to save up for the splurge."

"Oh Brad, that's awesome," Haylie said. "I hope everything works out for you and Sue. I really do!"

"Thanks Haylie." He closed out the browser and stepped aside so that she could sit down.

Pulling up a new browser, Haylie looked at the many icons that were scattered all over the desktop. She right-clicked on the screen, selected auto-arrange, and smiled as the icons neatly lined up in vertical rows down the left side of the computer.

***

Mid-way through the morning, Miriam decided it was time for a break. In the break room, she sat down at the computer and reached for the mouse, eager to play a few games of Solitaire. She went to click the icon, only to find that it wasn't there anymore.

In fact, none of the icons were where they were supposed to be! They used to be scattered all over the computer screen, and as untidy as it may have looked, Miriam knew exactly where to find whatever it was that she needed.

Now, Solitaire was nowhere to be found. What had happened?

Then she realized that the icons had somehow been neatly arranged in rows on the left side of the computer.

She didn't have to ask who had done it.

She already knew.

"HAYLIE!" She cried out at the top of her lungs.

Haylie promptly appeared in the break room. "What's wrong?" She asked.

"I'll tell you what's wrong," Miriam sneered, "You screwed up the computer! What gave you the right to think that you could do this?"

"I didn't screw up the computer!" Haylie responded angrily. "I auto-arranged the icons, that's all!"

"Well you better know how to undo it!"

Haylie put her hands on her hips. "And why should I?"

"Because I was here long before you, you little idiot! You think you can just march onto this nursing unit and take over? Start doing everything your way, eh? Did I miss something, or do the incompetent now reign supreme?"

"You're a witch," Haylie retorted. "You're a mean, fat, evil witch!

I've tried so hard to get along with you, but you've made me regret every nice thing I've ever done for you!"

Miriam stood up from her chair. "What do you think you've done for me, Haylie? Because I'll tell you what you've done for me. You've practically doubled my workload. I'm not only having to take care of my patients, but yours as well because you don't know what you're doing half the time! You've mocked me by calling me names behind my back. Don't think that I don't know about the whole 'Large Marge' thing. And what about the devil poster in the bathroom that you wrote my name on? I know that was you, Haylie! You've stressed me out to the point that I had an anxiety attack and ended up in the Emergency Department once already. Do you want to see me go back again? What are you trying to do, Haylie, kill me? Why don't you tell me again how many nice things you've done for me? Do I need to keep going?"

Tears poured down Haylie's cheeks. "Is that really what you think of me, Miriam? Do you really not see how hard I've been trying to do everything just right, so you won't be mad at me and we can get along?"

Miriam didn't respond. Her face was slowly turning red.

"I'm through here," Haylie said. "I quit." She ripped off her name badge and threw it onto the table in the break room. "You win, Miriam."

***

As Haylie rushed into Donna's office, she broke down and cried harder than she had in years.

"Don't quit," Donna said. "Please don't quit. We need you here."

"No you don't," Haylie said. "If you needed me that bad, then you wouldn't assign a preceptor to me who's determined to rip me to shreds every chance she can get."

Donna put her hand on Haylie's shoulder. "Let me talk to Miriam."

"You've been talking to her nonstop since I came to work here. She's sick of being talked to, and so am I. Nothing's ever going to change, Donna. If this is what it means to be a nurse, then I don't want to do it anymore."

"Haylie, please. Please don't quit. I'll find you a new preceptor if that's what it takes. Or maybe we can get you moved to another unit and you can start fresh somewhere else."

"Why do I have to leave? Why can't Miriam? She's the one who's causing all of the problems."

Donna shook her head from side to side. "Careful now," she cautioned. "You can't make Miriam the scapegoat. She can't be responsible for everything that's going wrong between the two of you. Do I need to remind you of the devil poster? Or the Large Marge comments?"

"Yeah, but that's nothing compared to what she's done to me!" Haylie cried out. "It's not fair! She can dish it out, but she can't take it?"

"Remember the class we all went to?" Donna asked. "The only nurse's behavior that you can be responsible for is your own. You must be the change you wish to see in the world."

Haylie blotted her eyes on a tissue. "So what does that mean… I have to be Miriam's doormat?"

"No," Donna replied. "I told you, we can find a new preceptor if that's what it takes. I recognize that Miriam hasn't always been fair and supportive of you. But at least give me a chance to make things better. Can you please do that, Haylie?"

She sat quietly for a moment, and then nodded.

"So you promise – you won't quit on me just yet, right?"

Haylie nodded. "Okay. I'll stay and give it another chance. But if it doesn't get better soon, I will resign, Donna. I'm serious about that."

Donna hugged her. "I'm sorry it's been a rocky start," she said. "But I'm going to do everything within my power to make it better for you. Besides… you can't quit right now. Employee appreciation days start tomorrow. Have you heard about them yet?"

Haylie shrugged. "I've seen some posters up around the hospital, but I haven't paid much attention to them."

"You're in for the time of your life," Donna said. "You'll be glad you chose to stay."

Chapter 17
Friday

Dogwood Regional Hospital's annual employee appreciation festival wasn't the typical, run-of-the-mill hospital celebration, according to Donna and Mel.

"You have no idea how lucky you are to work in a place like this," Donna insisted to Haylie. "Guess what they did for us on employee appreciation day at the last hospital where I worked? We got our choice of a free hot dog or hamburger, and a canned drink in the cafeteria. One free fast-food lunch in exchange for all that I did for that organization. That's all."

Mel raised a pointed finger at Donna as if to scold her. "Well that's better than what they did for me at MY last hospital. I got a plastic mug with their logo on it. Woohoo! Nothing says "you're appreciated" like a plastic mug. For crying out loud, you can't even put coffee in a plastic mug."

Haylie laughed at the two of them, although she did appreciate the point that they both were making. Dogwood Regional had contracted for private use of the state's largest amusement park for several days, and chartered several buses to transport the employees to and from.

Haylie had signed up for the first bus out of Dogwood on the first day of the event, determined to be number one in line to claim a little stress relief and fun that she was certainly entitled to. What she hadn't counted on was all of her co-workers coming along on the same bus.

Donna, Mel and Brad, she certainly didn't mind. But when Haylie saw Miriam step onto the bus, she literally felt nauseated. She sank down into her seat, hoping Miriam wouldn't see her. Maybe they could just avoid each other the whole bus trip, and certainly at the amusement park, Haylie hoped.

That hope was quickly crushed when Donna stood up and waved to Miriam, beckoning her to the back of the bus. Quickly switching seats to avoid having an empty space next to her, Haylie sat next to Brad, pinching her nose as she settled into the aisle seat across from the toilet.

***

When the bus pulled into the amusement park parking lot, the five nurses from Med-Surg South were the last to step out. Donna, Mel and Brad were glad that the long ride was over. Although not a word had been spoken between Haylie and Miriam, the long sighs and cold stares at each other made the tension palpable for all.

Brad and Haylie walked side by side, with Mel keeping pace behind them, and Donna and Miriam following in the rear. They all seemed to be in agreement – that they were here to have fun, for Pete's sake – but it wasn't going to happen as long as Miriam and Haylie were anywhere near each other.

They walked through the gates, showed their employee ID badges, and each received an armband that allowed them unlimited admission to all of the rides and attractions in the park throughout the day.

The very first ride beyond the gates was the infamous Rock'n'Roller Coaster. The line was one of the shorter ones, as the coaster had a reputation for being extremely scary and too intense. Last summer, Donna's children had warned her about the 'Puke'n'Roller Coaster' after a church youth group trip to the park.

One by one, without any thought or hesitation, the five nurses boldly marched into the line.

Brad looked around nervously.

"What's the matter?" Haylie asked, sensing his shaken nerves.

"Don't tell me you're afraid of roller coasters! Mister big strong Navy veteran… you, of all people?"

Blushing, he looked away. "Don't tell anyone. Please. I rode this same roller coaster at last year's employee appreciation day and I ended up throwing up as soon as I made it off the ride."

She smirked. "Your secret is safe with me. I despise roller coasters, too."

"So why are you in line?"

Haylie glanced over her shoulder at Miriam standing behind her, and then whispered as not to be overhead. "Miriam's going to ride it. I can't NOT ride it if she's going to."

"What?" Brad whispered back to her. "That's the dumbest thing I've ever heard."

"If I don't ride it, I'll look like a wimp, and I just can't give her one more thing to pick on me about. She's already called me stupid and incompetent and too young to know what I'm doing. I can't let her think I'm scared of a roller coaster."

The line moved, and the five of them advanced several steps.

Mel watched the roller coaster fly over her head, winding around the corkscrew track, and then making a loop-de-loop before plummeting toward the ground. Everyone on the coaster was screaming at the top of their lungs, loudly enough to drown out the sound of the rock'n'roll music blaring out the speakers mounted along the roller coaster tracks. In spite of all the noise, she could still hear Miriam breathing loudly, the way she always did when she was nervous and upset. Glancing at Miriam, she could see that her cheeks were flushed.

"Are you okay?" Mel asked. "You look a little red in the face."

Miriam's jaw tightened. "I'm just fine, she said through pursed lips."

Donna turned around, overhearing their conversation, and touched Miriam's face, more like a concerned mother than a nurse. "Are you sure? Don't want to see you have another episode and end up going back to Dogwood in an ambulance…"

"I'm just fine," Miriam shot back, brushing Donna's hand away. "I just hate roller coasters, that's all."

The line moved again, and they shuffled forward.

Donna's eyes grew wide. "Well then you're in the wrong line. You should probably get out of here and go find something else to do."

"No way," Miriam replied, without hesitating. "I'm riding this roller coaster if it kills me."

"And that's what I'm worried about. What if it does kill you? With your recent health problems, maybe you should rethink this," Mel pleaded, with genuine concern.

Miriam laughed gruffly. "It's a risk I'm willing to take."

Shrugging, Donna faced away from her. "I don't know why, but hey, it's your life."

Miriam didn't reply at first, but after a moment, she leaned forward and whispered to the two of them. "It's because Haylie's doing it," she said. "If Haylie's going to ride it, then I have to ride it, too."

"Are you crazy?" Mel asked.

Donna put her hands on her hips, ready to scold. "You think you're competing with her?"

"I'm not competing with her, no. I just don't want her to think that I can't handle it. She's already called me fat, and the devil, and who knows what else behind my back. So I can't let her think that I'm a wimp either. Can't give her any more ammunition to use against me."

Mel clapped her hand onto her forehead. "You're killing me, Miriam. This is ridiculous."

The line moved again, and suddenly, they were standing in front of a miniature train full of empty seats.

"Oh no," Haylie and Miriam said in unison.

The ride attendant waved them forward. "Two to a seat. Put on your seat belt and keep your hands and feet inside the car."

Brad looked at the ride and his face turned a ghostly shade of white. "Ugh," he said, "I don't think I can do this again. Sorry." He spun around and headed toward a stairwell with a "Coward's Exit" sign posted above it.

Haylie quickly grabbed Mel's arm. "Ride with me?" she pleaded.

"Sure," Mel agreed.

The attendant stepped forward. "Actually, no, you can't ride together." He pointed to Haylie, and then to Miriam. "You two are going to have to ride together."

"WHAT?" They both asked, looking at each other, and then at the attendant.

"Sorry," he said. "I have to balance the weight as equally as I can in the cars."

Haylie tried not to smile, but was unsuccessful. *Hah! Take that, fat old Miriam! What a slap in the face to you! I count for half a person, you count for one and a half!*

"No," Miriam said sharply. "I'm not riding with her."

Donna and Mel looked at each other and grinned.

"You know," Mel said, "I think Brad has the right idea. I don't think I'm going to ride today either." She made her way toward the stairs.

Donna was on her heels. "Me too. Have fun, ladies!" She called out to Miriam and Haylie, smiling over her shoulder.

The attendant was growing irritated. "Okay, you better get on or get off. I can't hold up the ride any longer."

Miriam and Haylie glared at each other.

"Fine by me… Airhead," Miriam relented.

"Let's do this then… Fatty," Haylie retorted.

They stumbled into the car, elbowing each other sharply as they buckled their seatbelts. The ride attendant pulled the metal safety bar down onto their laps.

"I hope what little bitty brain you have in your head doesn't get knocked out on this ride," Miriam said to her.

Haylie pretended to laugh. "I hope you stroke out and die," she said.

"I probably will," replied Miriam. "Because other than me, there aren't any real nurses on this ride. So there's no one to take care of me in the event that I do."

As all the other riders had settled in already, the attendant gave the thumbs up to his counterpart at the control panel. There was a loud buzz overhead, and the Rock'n'Roller Coaster was on the move.

ClackClackClackClackClackClackClack went the little train on the tracks, as it climbed up a steep hill...

"Hey," Haylie shouted, "I'm a REAL NURSE, Miriam... I passed my boards, just like you did... way back when dinosaurs roamed the earth, don't you remember?"

"Hah! What do you know about dinosaurs? You probably can't even spell the word 'dinosaur'..."

ClackClackClackClackClackClackClack...

"Why would I need to be able to spell 'dinosaur?' I mean, they're extinct aren't they? And isn't that because you ate them all, Porky?"

Miriam snorted loudly. "Wow! Aren't you clever? That's pretty original to call a fat woman 'Porky.' I'm impressed Haylie, really. As a matter of fact, I think I'll get it tattooed on one of my butt cheeks. And then wear pants that barely cover my bottom to work so I can show it off to everyone!"

ClackClackClackClackClackClackClack...

"Oh, don't flatter yourself. Our patients would stab their eyes out with the plastic forks on the food trays if they got one glance of your huge butt up on the unit!"

"Well Haylie, given the choice between seeing my fat behind walk through the door or your little skinny one, I think that any patient with half a brain is going to choose me as their nurse. I'd rather be old and fat than as stupid and incompetent as you any day of the week! You're ridiculous!"

As soon as the words had left her mouth, Miriam knew that she had crossed a line. Donna had been right all this time! She was being a bully.

She braced herself and waited for Haylie to respond, but the younger nurse didn't. Miriam turned her head slightly and saw that Haylie's eyes were wide, and her mouth was gaping open.

Whoooooooooooooooooooooooooooooooooooooooooshhhhhhhh...

Down the steep slope of the roller coaster they went. Held in place only by a rickety-looking metal bar across their laps and two flimsy orange seatbelts, Miriam and Haylie shrieked in unison as their rear ends simultaneously popped up slightly off their seats.

The coaster reached the bottom of the slope, twisted slightly to the right, and immediately climbed up another incline. This one, twice as tall, twice as steep....

ClackClackClackClackClackClackClack...

Still screaming, Haylie and Miriam looked at each other.

ClackClackClackClackClackClackClack...

"Oh my God... I think I'm going to be the one who dies on this thing!" Haylie said between screams.

ClackClackClackClackClackClackClack...

"I think I peed in my pants!" Miriam cried out.

Whoooooooooooooooooooooooooooooooooooooooshhhhhhh...

Down they went again, screaming the whole way.

And up they went again, into a long, winding corkscrew, through three sets of loop-de-loops, screaming all the way...

And finally, there they were at the beginning of the third and final incline, the highest, the steepest, and the most nausea-inducing part of the ride.

ClackClackClackClackClackClackClack...

"I think I peed in my pants too!" Haylie screamed.

"I don't think... I KNOW I peed in MY pants!" Miriam shrieked.

"Is that why the seat is wet? I thought it was me!"

"Well be thankful that it's just pee right now – it might be even worse when we get to the bottom of this one!"

ClackClackClackClackClackClackClack...

Then Miriam heard something – over the rock'n'roll music, and the screaming - that she thought was laughter.

Haylie's laughter.

She glanced out of the corner of her eye at Haylie, and indeed she was laughing. So hard that tears were streaming down her cheeks.

ClackClackClackClackClackClackClack...

And Miriam began to laugh too.

She laughed so hard that soon she had tears of her own spilling from her eyes.

ClackClackClackClackClackClackClack...

They reached the top of the slope, and there was a brief pause, a brief moment of calm before the rush downward. And the strangest thing happened in that moment.

Haylie reached over and grabbed Miriam's hand and squeezed it tightly.

And Miriam squeezed right back, as hard as she could.

It was also in that moment, that for some reason unknown to her, Miriam thought about Homer, and wondered if he could see her right then. If he was sitting up there in heaven, perched on a cloud, then surely she was high enough in the sky at the top of the roller coaster that he could see her up close at that moment.

What in the world would he say if he could see her? There she was, sitting in a rickety little roller coaster car, laughing so hard that she was crying (well, crying and wetting her pants), and holding on for dear life to the young woman whom she had made her enemy from the very moment that they had met. A young woman whom she blamed for her recent blood pressure problems and her red-faced spells of anger. A young nurse whom she knew deserved to be treated with kindness and respect, but for whatever reason, she was so emotionally spent that she didn't have it to give. What in the world would he say?

In a moment of clarity, Miriam knew exactly what Homer would say. And since he wasn't there, she said it for him, as she and Haylie plummeted down the slope at 60 plus miles per hour...

"Ohhh Thiiiiitt!!!"

Whoooooooooooooooooooooooooooooooooooooooooshhhhhhh...

And just like that, it was over.

They coasted back onto the wooden platform, from where they had boarded the ride just three minutes ago.

Miriam and Haylie were still clinging to each other. They sat quietly for a moment, their eyes wide open and their jaws dropped practically to their laps. They remained that way until the attendant came around, lifted the safety bar across their laps and unbuckled their seat belts.

Slowly, they stood up, smoothing their hair with their hands as they stepped off of the ride. Quietly, they made their way across the exit platform to the staircase.

"Hey, pass me the paper towels," they heard the attendant call out behind them, to his co-worker at the control panel, "We had a wetter here."

And suddenly Miriam and Haylie were seized with laughter again. They doubled over, blocking traffic as other riders tried to make their way around them and down the stairs.

***

Donna, Mel and Brad found Miriam and Haylie on a bench just outside of the Rock'n'Roller Coaster entrance, looking dazed and shaken. Yet strangely enough, they were both grinning.

"Did you have a nice ride, ladies?" Donna asked.

"It was…" Haylie searched for the right words.

"Interesting, to say the least," Miriam interjected. She tried not to smile, but couldn't help it.

"Actually I was going to say 'wet'," Haylie said, and laughed softly.

Mel cocked her head and smiled. "I can hardly believe what I'm seeing," she said. "The two of you… sitting here on this bench together, not bickering at each other for a change, and actually looking like you're having fun."

Brad shook his head. "I know. I'm having a hard time believing it too. I need someone to pinch me, because I think I'm dreaming."

Obliging him, Mel pinched him on his arm.

"Ow!" He cried out. "I wasn't being serious!"

"So I'll make it up to you," Mel grinned. "Come on, I'll go ride one of the kiddie rides with you since you're too scared to ride the grown-up ones. Your pick."

Brad rolled his eyes. "Whatever," he said, "I guess I can give the kiddie coaster a try." They linked arms and left, fighting their way through the growing crowd of Dogwood employees to the children's area of the park.

Donna remained, smiling down at Haylie and Miriam on the bench. "So ladies, you know what they say. Every moment is a teachable moment. What is it that you've learned from your roller coaster ride?"

Haylie and Miriam looked at each other, then back at Donna, confusion apparent on both of their faces.

"Well," Donna began, "I'll tell you what you learned. You need each other. And you'll never get through all the ups and downs if you can't lean on each other from time to time."

Miriam threw her hand up defensively. "Oh... not now, Donna. Take your roller coaster metaphors and go share some insightful life lessons with someone else."

"For real," Haylie agreed. "The only thing I can think about right now is trying not to barf."

Donna cocked one eyebrow. "Okay," she said. "Brush me off now if you want. But I know you two are hearing me, and you both know I'm right. And I've got proof that I'm right."

Neither of them made any comment in response.

Then, Donna reached into a large envelope that she had tucked under her arm. She drew out a photo and showed it to them.

"No you didn't," Haylie gasped.

"My Lord," Miriam said at the same time, cupping her hand over her mouth.

Donna tucked the picture back in the bag. "Bet you didn't realize that the amusement park has a camera mounted at the bottom of that third big drop on the roller coaster. The infamous "coaster cam"... takes a picture of you, right at the scariest moment of the ride. Great shot of you two hanging onto each other for dear life. I really just love it. Best ten dollars I ever spent. I think I'm going to frame it and hang it in the break room." Donna walked away with a satisfied smirk on her face.

"Hey Donna," Miriam called out to her, as she stood and smacked her hand onto her rear end, "Talk to the booty, 'cause this nurse is off duty."

"Hallelujah," Haylie moaned, just before she leaned forward and threw up on the ground.

***

That night, Miriam had a dream.

Journeying back into her past, she was twenty years old again. Young and vibrant and lovely, with long blonde hair, and slender hips. She was a new nurse – just out of nursing school, bright-eyed, fresh-faced, and ready to save the world.

She wore a long white dress, which was starched and ironed; not a crease or wrinkle to be found upon it. A blue cape draped around her shoulders. Her knee-high white stockings were a bit uncomfortable with the elastic band that pinched the back of her legs, and her lace-up white shoes weren't the most beautiful ones that she had ever seen, but still, she was proud of how professional she looked. After she had pinned on her nurse's cap, she stared at herself in the mirror for what felt like hours that morning, on the first day of her new job. Her name tag displayed her maiden name, the same one that was printed on her diploma when she had graduated just weeks before.

Miriam Rutter, Registered Nurse.

The words echoed throughout her mind like church bells ringing on Sunday morning.

Out the door she walked, almost two full miles, from the new nurse's dormitory to Our Lady of Mercy, a large Catholic hospital for indigent people. Most of the caregivers were also nuns, but the large volume of patients had recently led the hospital to begin hiring greater numbers of nurses from outside of the church.

Miriam reported to the third floor sick ward, to the head nurse, Sister Mary Charles. The aging nun was short, stout and hard-faced. While the nuns around her looked like angels in their flowing white habits, there was nothing heavenly about Sister Mary Charles. Her voice was gruff, her steps were loud and heavy and her demeanor was impatient and unkind.

Yet, Miriam remained positive and hopeful, and was thrilled when she was assigned her first patient. Sister Mary Charles walked her through the ward, which was separated from the rest of the third floor by a single yellow curtain. Weaving their way around cots that were placed closely together, they arrived at the bedside of an elderly man who was napping.

"This is bed fourteen. Amputation of the right leg, just below the knee, due to a foot injury that turned into gangrene." Miriam could see the discomfort on his face when Sister Mary Charles lifted the blanket to check on his stump, awakening him from a peaceful, pain-free sleep. "This is your first patient, Miriam Rutter," she'd said. "Bed fourteen."

Miriam looked into the Sister's eyes. "What is his name?"

She glared back at Miriam. "Bed fourteen," she said. "Didn't you hear me the first two times? You will refer to him as bed fourteen."

The old man's eyes fluttered open. "My name," he said softly, "is Andrew McHugh, and I need to make water."

The Sister stepped away from his bed, pointing at Miriam. "This is your nurse. She will help you with that."

Miriam blushed. She had never seen a man in the nude before – only in her textbooks. The idea of taking off Mr. McHugh's pants suddenly made her very nervous, and she froze.

Sister Mary Charles lifted an eyebrow. "Didn't you hear him? He needs to pass urine. Get his bedpan. It's under his bed." She tapped her foot on the floor.

Obligingly, young Miriam knelt below the bed and retrieved his bedpan. Next, she stood up and placed it on the corner of his bed. She reached toward Mr. McHugh to unfasten his pants, and then hesitated. She looked up at Sister Mary Charles, pleading with her eyes for guidance and help.

Unfortunately, there was none available. "Go on," she barked at Miriam, "take care of your patient!"

Miriam rolled Mr. McHugh's pants down his thighs, and then his underwear. She carefully positioned his blanket to try to preserve his privacy, and then slid the bedpan under his buttocks. He relieved himself for a long, long time.

When he was done, Miriam slid the bedpan out from under her patient. His urine was dark and smelly, and the bedpan was very full. She lifted it from the bed with as much caution as she could, giving great care to not spill a drop.

And then, without warning, Mr. McHugh began to cough. His body lifted up from off the bed for a split second, and his elbow tapped the bedpan. A small bit of urine splashed onto his bed, and down onto the bandage of his stump.

Sister Mary Charles looked at Miriam, her eyes growing wide. "Fool," she growled, "you've contaminated his dressing. Now it has to be done all over again."

Then she reached out and took the bedpan away from Miriam. "So you like to spill urine on your patients? Why don't you see how it feels?" She tilted the bedpan forward, dumping hot urine all over Miriam's uniform. It soaked through to her chest and flowed down past her waist, her legs, all the way to her feet, soaking into her shoes.

"Clean up this mess," the Sister ordered, pointing to the urine on the floor. "There's a cleaning closet in the back of the ward. You'll find mops in there. And then go bathe yourself. Don't come back until you're ready to be a good nurse."

With tears spilling down her cheeks, Miriam pushed past Sister Mary Charles and went to find a mop. She made her way to the cleaning closet, stepped inside, and cried for several moments. She wasn't prepared to come out just yet when she heard a soft knock on the door. Miriam ignored it, hoping that whoever it was would go away.

But the knock came again, so she relented, and slowly opened the door. Another nun stood before her, wearing a gentle smile on her face. "I'm Sister Agnes," she said. "If you will hand me a mop, I will clean the floor for you."

Hesitantly, Miriam passed her a mop. "Won't Sister Mary Charles be mad?"

"Perhaps. But I'm sure there will come a day when I'll have a mess of my own that you will clean up for me. Surely she'll understand that."

Sister Agnes left with the mop and returned a few minutes later. Recognizing her knock on the door, Miriam answered.

"I have a coat that you can wear, if you'd like to take off your uniform and carry it back to the dorm with you instead of wearing it." She reached into the closet and handed Miriam a long, green button-down coat. "It will cover you from head to toe," Sister Agnes said.

Miriam took the jacket. "Thank you," she said softly.

"And here is a sheet, for you to wrap your uniform in until you can clean it. And also… I prepared a warm washcloth for you, so you can clean yourself a bit. Just until you can get to a shower." She smiled, even more kindly than before, as she handed the other items to Miriam.

"Thank you," Miriam repeated.

Sister Agnes closed the door and gave Miriam a moment to clean up and change into the green coat. Then she reached in and took Miriam by the hand. "You can come out now. Don't be afraid." She pulled her out of the closet, hooked her arm into Miriam's, and walked by her side through the ward. Back through the curtain they went, down two flights of stairs, and then out of the hospital.

They had passed by Sister Mary Charles in the ward, but she paid no attention to either of them.

It was as if Miriam had an angel by her side.

"How can I thank you?" she asked Sister Agnes.

The nun smiled again. "Just don't give up, Miriam. Come back tomorrow. And the next day. And the next." She put her arms around the young nurse and hugged her tightly.

And when Miriam pulled back from Sister Agnes' embrace, she found that something strange had happened. It was as if her dream was unfolding as a scene in a play, and the characters had somehow shuffled onstage. In the new arrangement, Miriam had taken the place of Sister Agnes. She was wearing the nun's white habit, a much bigger habit than the one that Sister Agnes had worn. Bigger, and a bit longer to cover her wide hips – her hips? She looked down, and her body was no longer young; her girlish figure was gone. The dream had changed. She was no longer Miriam past, but Miriam present once again.

And the young nurse standing before her was no longer herself.

It was Haylie. In a long, button-down green coat, with tear stained cheeks, smelling of urine…

But smiling back at her nonetheless.

"How can I thank you?" Haylie asked.

Miriam swallowed hard, feeling a knot in her throat. "Just come back tomorrow. And I promise… I'll be different from now on, Haylie, I will be your angel. I promise … I promise… "

Miriam began to weep. She leaned forward and took Haylie into her arms, embracing her tightly. Sorrow flowed freely from her eyes, and in her heart she begged for forgiveness and understanding.

"How can I thank you?" Haylie asked her again.

"Just don't give up, Haylie. We need you. So come back tomorrow," said Miriam. "And the next day. And the next."

Chapter 18
The Next Monday

That morning, Miriam came into work early. She went into the break room, where she placed a small gift bag on the table. Then she walked out into the unit and took a stroll through the rooms to peek in on the patients.

Mr. Crowell was back, after having had another surgery, and asking for pain medication already. Mr. Eldridge was still in his room, sleeping soundly. Ms. Burton had been discharged sometime yesterday while they had been at the amusement park. In her place was a new patient, a teenage boy, who had been in a motorcycle accident. He had suffered multiple injuries and had undergone surgery last night to have pins put in his left arm and leg. Miriam started to walk past his room, but stopped herself. She poked her head in the room and greeted the boy's mother, who sat by his bedside while he slept.

"Good morning," Miriam whispered.

"Good morning," the tired-looking woman replied.

"What's your young man's name?" Miriam asked.

"Ralph James," she said, "but just keep in mind, he goes by 'Junior' since his dad is named Ralph also."

Miriam smiled. "Junior," she said.

Upon hearing his name, his eyes opened and he focused his attention on Miriam.

"Good morning," she said. "Your nurse today will be Haylie. She's a great nurse. You and your mom will like her a lot."

***

When Haylie arrived on Med-Surg South that morning, she was still smiling over the events of the weekend. Isabel's wedding had been the most beautiful, perfect ceremony that Haylie had ever seen. Even Dan thought so. The two of them had danced the night away at the reception under the starry sky on the outdoor patio of the country club. Haylie wasn't surprised when the night ended with a kiss and plans for a real date – just the two of them – for the following weekend.

She was so excited and delighted by the unexpected romance with Dan that even the return to work that morning couldn't take the grin off her face. She was ready to take on the day, whatever it had in store for her; whatever kind of sabotage Miriam had planned for her next.

Haylie clocked in and went into the break room to stash her lunch bag in the refrigerator. She almost didn't see the gift bag sitting on the break room table. The card attached to it had her name on it, which caught her eye just before she left the room. She sat down to read it.

Dear Haylie,

She immediately recognized the handwriting as Miriam's. Surprised and curious, she read on.

I've never been good with words. As you know I sometimes… well, I OFTEN say the wrong thing. I don't want to do that this time, which is why I'm taking the time to sit down and sort out my thoughts, and finally, put them on paper. I know that I haven't been the best colleague and mentor to you, and I have to apologize for that. I hope that you will bear with me as I work on doing a better job at it.

I never thanked you for coming to Homer's visitation and funeral. Nor did I thank you for coming to my rescue when I felt ill last week. I didn't realize it at the time, but you were there for me, and it truly means a lot. I do thank you – now and always – and hope you will believe just how much I appreciate what you have done for me.

Haylie, I have to be honest with you. You are NOT a good nurse.

You are far better than just a good nurse.

You are an EXCELLENT nurse.

You have a lot to learn (and I hope to be able to help you with that), but you already have the single most important thing that it takes to be a nurse – your amazing, caring heart.

There is a gift for you in this bag. It's an angel for you to wear on your shoulder. Since you have been an angel to me, I am asking you to wear this so that every time I see you, I will remember that it is now my turn to be an angel to you.

Sincerely,

Miriam

Haylie reached into the bag and pulled out a jewelry box. Lifting the cover, she found a beautiful lapel pin resting on a square of cotton. It was a small cluster of pearls and crystals, shaped into an angel. A tiny gold halo rested on its head.

She read Miriam's note again, and without thinking twice, fastened the pin to her collar.

***

Finding Miriam on the floor, Haylie reached out and hugged her. Miriam hugged back.

"Miriam, thank you for the pin. It's gorgeous and I'd be happy to wear it."

"Thank you, Haylie. I really appreciate that."

Haylie looked down and touched the pin. "I'm… I'm really sorry for a lot of the things that I've said and done. I know I've acted childishly at times, I hope you'll forgive me, too."

"It's okay," Miriam said. "I know that a lot of what you did was just in reaction to my own words and actions. I have a responsibility to you, to be a mentor and a role model. I haven't done a great job so far, but that's going to change."

She smiled. "Thanks Miriam. That means a lot to me."

"It's not always going to come naturally for me, you know. I'll need for you to help hold me accountable. The class that we took … I know I was really sarcastic and mouthy about it at the time, but what we learned was actually good stuff. And I'm expecting you to confront me if there's ever a time when you feel like I'm not being fair or appropriate, or supporting you in your work."

"It goes both ways," Haylie said, nodding. "In fact, we all need to do that for each other. Mel and Donna and Brad and everyone else on our unit, all of us. We need to hold ourselves and each other accountable."

"You're right," Miriam nodded. "Maybe if we start, everyone else will follow our lead."

"I'm certainly willing to give it a shot."

"Give what a shot?" Donna asked, as she walked onto the unit.

"You'll see, soon enough," Miriam said, winking at Haylie.

"What's this? The two of you conspiring together?" Donna wrinkled her brow with mock worry. "I'm just starting to wonder if maybe that roller coaster ride shook the common sense out of you."

"Nah," Haylie said. "I think it actually did the opposite."

"Well that's good to hear," Donna said, "Because I want you both to go back after work today."

"What?" Haylie and Miriam asked at the same time.

"The park is still open for Dogwood employees tonight. Today's the last day of Employee Appreciation Days, and the last bus leaves at 7:30, so I expect you two to be on it."

"But we already went," Miriam protested. "Aren't we only supposed to go once?"

"I'm your boss," Donna said firmly, "and this is an order. You two have been stressing me out for way too long. You work too hard and take yourselves too seriously! You're more alike than you know, and you both need to lighten up and have more fun. It makes you better people. I want you both to be on that bus at 7:30."

"Can't argue with that," Haylie said.

Miriam shrugged. "You're the boss. We'll be on the bus."

***

Inside the park, Haylie and Miriam went straight to the Rock'n'Roller Coaster line. They moved through it fairly quickly, and the attendant even remembered them from the Friday before. He put them in the front car this time.

ClackClackClackClackClackClackClack...

Whooooooooooooooooooooooooooooooooooooshhhhhhh...

ClackClackClackClackClackClackClack...

Whooooooooooooooooooooooooooooooooooooshhhhhhh...

Corkscrew...

Loop-de-loop, loop-de-loop, loop-de-loop

ClackClackClackClackClackClackClack...

And there they were again, making the incline up the steepest, scariest slope, the grand finale to the whole ride. They braced themselves as they dipped over the top, and then, all too fast, they were coasting down....

Whooooooooooooooooooooooooooooooooooooshhhhhhh...

Only this time, Haylie was watching for the flash of the camera. She was determined to look not quite so crazed and frightened this time when the coaster cam took a picture of her and Miriam. So she smiled, tried to narrow her eyes a bit so they didn't look like they were going to pop out of her head, and then it came, the *FLASH* that she hadn't even noticed last time.

She looked over at Miriam, wondering if she would be screaming or smiling in the picture this time.

And what she saw in that moment was something that she would later try, on many occasions, to describe to Brad and Mel and Donna, but would never quite be able to put into words.

When the camera flashed, it cast a brilliant light upon Miriam's face. It made her eyes look bluer than the sky, her face brighter than the sunshine, and her smile, more dazzling than Haylie had ever seen before.

The most amazing thing, though, was the way that the flash of light shone through Miriam's hair in that split second. It suddenly looked translucent, somewhat golden, almost glowing. It was shimmering. Sparkling. Blindingly bright, and indescribably beautiful.

Almost like a halo.

SUGGESTED READING LIST

Although this story about lateral violence in nursing is a work of fiction, you can find factual, evidence-based information about lateral violence in published sources, including professional nursing journals. Here are a few suggested resources to enhance your understanding of the concepts depicted in this novella:

Bartholomew, K. (March 2006). Ending nurse to nurse hostility: why nurses eat their young and each other. HCPro, Marblehead, MA

Griffin, M. (2004) Teaching cognitive rehearsal as a shield for lateral violence: an intervention for newly licensed nurses. Journal of Continuing Education for Nurses. 35 (6), 257-63.

Griffin, M. (2005) Awareness of nurse on nurse abuse helps resolve problem. AORN Management Connections. 5, 3-5.

Hawkins, A. & Kratsch, L. (2004). Troubled units: creating change. AACN Clinical Issues, 15(2), 215-221.

McKenna, B.G., Smith, N.A., Poole, S.J., (2003) Horizontal Violence: Experiences of registered nurses in their first year of practice. Journal of Advanced Nursing. 42, 90-96.

Roberts, S.J. (1983), "Oppressed group behaviour: implications for nursing", *Advances in Nursing Science*, Vol. 5 pp.21-30.

DISCUSSION GROUP QUESTIONS

1. Which character did you relate to the most and why?

2. Were there any specific situations in the story that you identified with? (Personal life issues, conflicts, patients, situations at work?)

3. How do the personal lives of the five nurses affect them at work?

4. How do you think that Haylie felt after her first day at work? How do you think Miriam felt after Haylie's first day at work?

5. How do you think that Brad feels being the only male nurse on Med-Surg South? Do you think that male nurses are affected differently by lateral violence than female nurses?

6. Identify and discuss specific acts of lateral violence that you can remember from the story. Next, think about acts of violence that have been committed against you by other nurses, and think about times when you have acted violently toward other nurses. Discuss if you are comfortable doing so (protecting the privacy of others. Do not identify others by name).

7. Who do you think felt the most powerless in the story? Where does power come from in nursing? Discuss a time when you felt powerless. Discuss a time when you felt powerful.

8. How do relationships between nurses and doctors affect a nurse's performance in the workplace? Do you remember a situation in the story in which a doctor helped a nurse? Or when a doctor hindered a nurse?

9. How are patients affected by lateral violence? Are there any situations in the story in which patients are exposed to violence among nurses?

10. Thinking about the class that the nurses attended, were you surprised to hear that there is a historical and cultural basis for lateral violence? Do you think that other professions in health care are equally impacted by lateral violence, or are nurses the group that is most affected?

11. Are you familiar with the term 'compassion fatigue?' (If not, a quick internet search should help you find some definitions of the term). What role does it play in lateral violence? What character do you think suffers most from compassion fatigue?

12. When Miriam experiences her turnaround and writes a note to Haylie to express her feelings, the story doesn't tell you how Haylie felt about it. How do you think she felt? How would you have felt, had you been in Haylie's position?

13. Thinking of the top ten acts of lateral violence, which ones are the most obvious and overt? Which are the ones that aren't as obvious? Are there acts of violence that are easy to commit without thinking about it?

14. Lateral violence is a learned behavior. Is there a point in which you see this happening in the story?

15. Read over the scripted responses to acts of lateral violence. How difficult would it be for you to begin using responses such as these? Create your own role play exercise with a fellow nurse like the one that Haylie and Laura used in the story and test out a rehearsed response to an act of lateral violence. Discuss with your peers.

POST-TEST QUESTIONS

Lions and Tigers and Nurses

1) Which of the following is not included in the top ten lateral violence behaviors?:

a) Infighting

b) Sabotage

c) Constructive Criticism

d) Backstabbing

e) Scapegoating

2) When Miriam told Haylie to call Dr. Fox and expected him to be angry with her, it was an example of:

a) Sabotage

b) Withholding Information

c) Non-verbal innuendo

d) Both a & b

e) Both b & c

3) When Haylie overheard two nurses talking about Brad and Mel in the elevator, she spoke up because she felt that the nurses were demonstrating a lateral violence act of:

a) Infighting

b) Non-verbal innuendo

c) Failure to respect privacy

d) Backstabbing

e) Broken confidence

4) A culture that is _____ will inevitably turn against itself.

   a) weak

   b) oppressed

   c) nursing

   d) violent

   e) uplifted

5) All of the following are examples of universally accepted working behaviors except:

   a) Accept your fair share of the work

   b) Don't publicly criticize others

   c) Let small conflicts go as it's best to avoid confrontation whenever you can

   d) Be respectful toward superiors

   e) Ask for help when you need it and help others when they ask for it

6) What is a common example of non-verbal innuendo in the workplace?

   a) Rolling eyes

   b) Giving someone a nickname

   c) Withholding important information about a patient

   d) Bickering with a peer

   e) Spreading rumors

7) The fact that Miriam was treated badly by her first mentor in nursing shows that:

   a) She repressed it until the memory of it came back to her in her dream

   b) She became a successful nurse in spite of the way that she was treated

   c) Lateral violence was more pronounced and more obvious many years ago

   d) Lateral violence is a learned behavior

   e) It is impossible to break the cycle of lateral violence

8) An effective verbal response to infighting might be:

   a) "I'm not continuing with this conversation until a manager is present."

   b) "I'm going to be the better person and just walk away."

   c) "Nobody's perfect. That includes you."

   d) "This isn't the time or the place to discuss this. We need to talk about this later."

   e) There is no effective verbal response to infighting.

9) Haylie backstabbed another nurse when she:

   a) Invited Dan to her sister's wedding while she assumed he was in a relationship with another person

   b) Confronted the two nurses in the elevator about them talking about Brad and Mel

   c) Complained to Mel in the break room about Miriam

   d) Used the technique that Miriam taught her to start an IV

   e) Auto-arranged the computer icons without realizing it would upset Miriam

10) Violence occurs:

    a) Only when there is bodily harm

    b) Only between nurses

    c) When someone's body, possessions, or feelings are harmed

    d) As a natural behavior

    e) Happens only between groups (ie, between physicians and nurses), not within groups

11) Which of the following statements are true about lateral violence?

    a) There is no historical basis for lateral violence in nursing; it is a relatively new phenomenon

    b) Male nurses are generally exempt from lateral violence

    c) Lateral violence is not part of the culture that nurses report as a reason that drives them to leave their jobs

    d) Lateral violence can be reduced or prevented with the use of rehearsed responses to violent behaviors

    e) Lateral violence is simply a rite of passage that all new nurses must endure as they transition into their nursing careers

12) If you overhear a group of nurses talking to each other about someone that is not present, you can intervene by:

    a) Doing nothing – ignore the behavior

    b) Point out the behavior to a nurse manager

    c) Speak up on behalf of the absent colleague and suggest to your peers that they not have discussions about the person unless they are present

    d) Tell the absent colleague about the conversation so that he or she can go to the group and deal with it directly

    e) Use non-verbal communication, such as rolling your eyes, to show that you disapprove

13) Your nurse manager called a meeting and announced it to everyone present on the nursing unit. One of your colleagues had left the unit to go get a cup of coffee when the meeting was announced. When she returns, you choose not to tell her about the meeting. This is an example of:

   a) Non-verbal innuendo

   b) Infighting

   c) Failure to respect privacy

   d) Undermining

   e) Withholding information

14) One of your colleagues spilled a cup of ice water on a patient. Your colleagues gave him the nickname "John The Baptist." This is an example of:

   a) Undermining

   b) Infighting

   c) Scapegoating

   d) Broken Confidence

   e) Sabotage

15) Another nurse approaches you in your patient's room and tells you that she's mad at you for a comment that you made earlier in the day. You should tell her:

   a) "Can't you see I'm taking care of a patient? Maybe you should go do the same thing."

   b) "This really isn't the right time or place to talk about this. I would be glad to talk with you privately in just a moment."

   c) "I'm not saying a word to you unless our boss is present. Maybe you should go get her."

   d) Don't say anything just yet. Leave the patient alone and go deal with your colleague's issue first.

   e) Don't say anything. Just ignore your colleague and don't make eye contact.

CONTINUING NURSING EDUCATION TEST

Lions and Tigers and Nurses

Instructions:

- After reading the novella, complete the post-test, the evaluation, and the registration form.
- Mail the completed documents with fee made to:
  Department of Nursing Continuing Education
  Southern Regional AHEC
  1601 Owen Drive
  Fayetteville, NC 28304
- Within 4-6 weeks after we receive your paperwork and with successful completion of the post-test, your continuing education certificate will be mailed to you. Passing score is 80%. If you fail, you have the option of retaking the test at no additional cost
- Questions? Contact SRAHEC Department of Nursing Continuing Education at 910-678-7216 or 910-678-7246.

Provider Accreditation (readers are eligible for 3 contact hours, CNE)

Southern Regional AHEC is approved as a provider of continuing nursing education by the North Carolina Nurses Association, an accredited approver by the American Nurses Credentialing Center's Commission on Accreditation.

AP#005-607

Payment

The registration fee for this test is $10.00 per person. Checks should be made payable to "Southern Regional AHEC". We also accept Visa and MasterCard. Do not send cash with your paperwork. Institutional/bulk discounts for ten or more tests are available. Please call 910-678-7216 for more information.

Purpose of this educational activity:

Lions and Tigers and Nurses is an educational fiction novella (short novel) about lateral violence in nursing culture. Through a fiction story, readers will meet a cast of 5 nursing characters at a hospital's Med-Surg unit. The newest nurse on the unit, Haylie, is paired with preceptor, Miriam, the most senior nurse on the unit. The relationship between the two nurses is high-conflict and marked by a number of laterally violent behaviors. The nurse manager, Donna, realizes that an intervention is needed and takes her team of nurses to a program on lateral violence. Together, the nurses learn about the history of lateral violence in nursing, the top ten behavioral manifestations of lateral violence, and interventions to reduce and stop lateral violence in the workplace. Self-study and reflective book discussion group questions are included in the story to validate learning.

Learning Objectives:

Upon completion of this educational activity, the participant should be able to:

1) Define lateral violence

2) Discuss why lateral violence occurs among nurses

3) List the top ten behavioral manifestations of lateral violence in the workplace

4) Identify evidence-based verbal responses to laterally violent behaviors

CNE ENROLLMENT FORM

Lions and Tigers and Nurses

CASCE # 26929

Please print or type. All fields must be completed in order to score the test and award continuing education credits. Incomplete enrollment forms will be returned.

Name _____

❑ RN   ❑ LPN   ❑ NP   ❑ CRNA   ❑ Student   ❑ Other _____

Address _____

Last 4 digits of SSN: XXX-XX- _____

City _____

State _____ Zip Code _____

Home Phone _____

Email _____

Employer _____

Job Title _____

Work Address _____

Area of Specialty _____

Work City _____

State _____ Zip Code _____

Work Phone _____

Work Email _____

Preferred mailing address to receive certificated of completion:
❑ work ❑ home

Amount enclosed $10.00 paid by:
❑ Check enclosed (made payable to "SRAHEC") ❑ MasterCard ❑ Visa

Credit card # _____

Signature _____

Last 3 digits on signature panel _____

TEST ANSWERS

Place an "X" through your answer to each question

1. A   B   C   D

2. A   B   C   D

3. A   B   C   D

4. A   B   C   D

5. A   B   C   D

6. A   B   C   D

7. A   B   C   D

8. A   B   C   D

9. A   B   C   D

10. A   B   C   D

11. A   B   C   D

12. A   B   C   D

13. A   B   C   D

14. A   B   C   D

15. A   B   C   D

ACTIVITY EVALUATION

1. The course content was pertinent to my educational needs
    and practice

❏ Strongly Agree   ❏ Agree   ❏ Neutral   ❏ Disagree Strongly
                        ❏ N/A   ❏ Disagree

2. Course objectives were met

❏ Strongly Agree   ❏ Agree   ❏ Neutral   ❏ Disagree Strongly
                        ❏ N/A   ❏ Disagree

3. I will be able to incorporate what I learned into my practice

❏ Strongly Agree   ❏ Agree   ❏ Neutral   ❏ Disagree Strongly
                        ❏ N/A   ❏ Disagree

Comments:_____

_____

_____

_____

_____

_____

Mail this form with your payment to:

> Department of Nursing Continuing Education
> Southern Regional AHEC
> 1601 Owen Drive
> Fayetteville, NC 28304